TENNIS
WITHOUT
LESSONS

JIM BROWN

McNeese State University

TENNIS
WITHOUT
LESSONS

PRENTICE-HALL, INC., Englewood Cliffs, N.J.

Library of Congress Cataloging in Publication Data

BROWN, JIM (date).
    Tennis without lessons.

    Bibliography: p.
    Includes index.
    SUMMARY: A guide for beginning and intermediate tennis
players using a teach-yourself approach. Discusses rules,
strokes, strategy, improving without playing, recognizing
and correcting problems, and playing intelligently.
    1. Tennis. [1. Tennis] I. Title.
GV995.B6928   796.34'22   76-18801
ISBN 0-13-903252-5

© 1977 by PRENTICE-HALL, INC.
Englewood Cliffs, New Jersey

Printed in the United States of America

10 9 8 7 6 5 4 3 2

PRENTICE-HALL INTERNATIONAL, INC., *London*
PRENTICE-HALL OF AUSTRALIA PTY. LIMITED, *Sydney*
PRENTICE-HALL OF CANADA, LTD., *Toronto*
PRENTICE-HALL OF INDIA PRIVATE LIMITED, *New Delhi*
PRENTICE-HALL OF JAPAN, INC., *Tokyo*
PRENTICE-HALL OF SOUTHEAST ASIA PTE. LTD., *Singapore*

Contents

v

Preface

The best way for most people to begin learning how to play tennis is to take lessons from qualified teaching professionals. These people make a living teaching tennis and can get you started correctly. However, for a variety of reasons, thousands of players do not take lessons. One problem is that there are not enough pros to meet the demand for lessons. There are approximately 35 million people playing tennis regularly in the United States today. If every state had 50 qualified professionals teaching full time, there would still be only one teacher for every 14,000 players. The teacher-to-player ratio in other parts of the world is even lower.

There are other reasons why tennis players do not take lessons. Some people cannot afford the prices that professionals must charge. Other players do not have access to qualified instructors because of location or club restrictions. Some tennis enthusiasts simply do not want to take lessons. Furthermore, very few people take lessons forever. After a series of lessons, they have heard all that the pro has to say and only go back for help when something is wrong with their game.

This book is written for all of those people who are learning to play tennis without formal instruction. While it may not be the best way, it is possible to learn the game on your own and to develop a high level of skill. You can also recognize and correct your own problems instead of paying someone to do it for you.

In the first chapter of *Tennis Without Lessons* you will get information on getting started in the game. Ideas on the benefits and risks of tennis, how good you can become, where and who you can play, and the buying of equipment and clothes are presented. Fifty of the most frequently asked questions about the rules of tennis are answered, and tennis terms are defined.

In the second chapter you will learn how each of the strokes in tennis should be hit, how you can teach yourself to play, and what to do when something goes wrong with part of your game.

You also have to know when and where to use certain strokes. The chapter on "Developing Strategy" gives you some strategic ideas for singles, doubles, and mixed doubles, and will help you figure out special court problems.

By now you know that tennis is a thinking person's game. The chapter entitled "Playing Intelligently" will give you something to think about in the areas of concentration, anticipation, tennis psychology, and the way to personalize your game.

You can also improve your game off of the court. Reading about tennis, observing it closely, and taking care of yourself physically are three ways to do so. These ways are explored in Chapter 5, "Improving Without Playing."

"Practicing," the last chapter, should help you practice more effectively. Solutions to such problems as not having enough time, not knowing how to practice, and not having anyone with whom to practice are given, as well as advice on how to practice at home.

People have learned to play sports throughout the history of the world without the benefit of professional instruction. Get help if you want it, need it, and can afford it, but do not let the lack of lessons keep you from playing and enjoying tennis throughout your life.

I would like to thank David Brown for taking the photographs in this book.

TENNIS
WITHOUT
LESSONS

1

Getting Started

BECOMING INVOLVED

What Is in It for You?

Before you decide that you are going to get serious about tennis, there are several things you should know about the sport. As with anything else, there are both benefits and risks that should be considered.

The advantages outweigh the disadvantages for most people, and there are some sound pro-tennis arguments. Tennis can be beneficial for health, family unity, and social purposes. It is a sport that can be enjoyed for a lifetime; it is cheap; and it is fun.

For promoting health and maintaining fitness, playing tennis is better for you than most sports. Golf, the sport most often compared with tennis, hardly satisfies the definition of exercise. Baseball, softball, and football not only are inadequate as methods of maintaining total fitness, they are impractical for many adults because they are seasonal activities and they require large groups of people for competition. Fishing, hunting, bowling, and walking may be entertaining, but their relationship to fitness is rather tenuous for most people. Running and swimming would earn more points on an exercise scale for intensity of effort required, but the boredom caused by the repetition turns off millions of Americans.

Tennis has attracted between 30 and 40 million people in the United States alone. These people burn as many as 500 calories an hour while playing, and their muscles become stronger without becoming much bigger. As a time-saving way to get exercise, playing tennis packs more movement into one hour than most sports do in three. You do not have to commit yourself for an entire day to get whatever it is you want from the sport. Many of the people who play tennis also feel better emotionally because the combination of continuous movement and hitting a tennis ball several hundred times in an hour appears to release tension.

Tennis can also be a nice way to promote family togetherness. You can play with or against your spouse and your children, and you can have just as much fun practicing with them as you can competing with them. If competitive tennis interests you, there are father-son tournaments, mother-daughter tournaments, husband-wife tournaments, parent-child tournaments, and probably tournaments for other family combinations. Family vacations can be spent in tennis resorts, tennis camps, or on tennis tournament circuits.

If you are interested in tennis for social purposes, the sport will enable you to meet a new group of people and make new friends. People in every special interest group have peculiar characteristics, and tennis players have a collective mind and a language all their own. The personalities range from the gym-shorted, beer-drinking public court players to the most sophisticated club types.

Tennis is a lifetime sport. Very young and very old people are playing every day. This is a sport to which people of all ages can adjust. The best professional players must maintain physical fitness levels comparable to those of athletes in basketball and track; but as the ordinary players get older, slower, and weaker, there are ways to play tennis according to their capabilities. The age groupings designated by national, state, and local tennis organizations make it possible for fair competition with people just as old, slow, and weak as you may be.

Tennis does not have to cost a lot of money. You could spend less than three dollars for a can of balls and ten dollars for a cheap racket and be ready to go. Compare those prices with the cost of golf clubs, hunting and fishing equipment, and health spa fees. The cost of playing tennis tends to increase as a player's skill level and interest increase, so a person could eventually spend a lot of money playing the game. More about that later. But large initial expenditures are not essential for enjoying tennis.

Finally, but most important of all the reasons for becoming involved in tennis: it is fun. Millions of Americans can't be wrong in this case. Argue the merits of other sports all you want, but playing tennis is more fun for most people than standing in right field for three hours, butting heads at left tackle, riding in an electric cart, or jogging through dog-infested neighborhoods. Tennis requires movement, skill, and a competitive spirit—a difficult combination to beat for sheer entertainment.

Are You Sure You Want to Become Involved?

For those people who are looking for a bridge club substitute, tennis may not be the best choice. It is a physically demanding game at most levels. Tennis probably requires a wider range of physical skills and mental alertness than most other sports. You do not have to be a great athlete to enjoy participation, but if you are thinking, "I've never been good at sports; maybe tennis is my game," think again. If you decide to play, make up your mind that you are going to run, work hard, perspire, and enjoy doing it.

Beginning players usually go out to the courts or watch tennis on television as they become interested in playing. The outstanding players seen in tournament tennis make it look so easy that the novice may assume the sport can be learned without difficulty. However, it is not an easy game to learn, especially if you plan to learn without the benefit of lessons. The beginner spends more time retrieving balls than hitting them. The problems created by trying to hit a small moving object into the proper court, while on the run and in various positions, are formidable. If you decide to play, accept the fact that although you can enjoy being a beginner, it is going to take years for you to achieve an advanced level of play.

You have been told what tennis does not have to cost you, but you should know that it can be expensive under certain circumstances. One expense can be in getting a court on which to play or practice. If you live in a part of the country where you cannot play outdoors all year, and if you want to play more than just during the summer months, you may have to rent an indoor court or join a club. There are two general types of indoor tennis operations. One type of club charges membership fees and monthly dues comparable to the cost usually associated with country clubs. The high price of club membership is offset somewhat by very nominal court fees or no court fees at all. In other words, you pay a lot for membership, but get free court time. The other type of club charges relatively little for individual or family memberships, but the cost of reserving a court is expensive. In metropolitan areas you may have to pay from ten to thirty dollars an hour for a court. Those prices can be cut in half if you share the cost with a friend, or the court fee can be split four ways if you have a doubles group.

Taking lessons can also be expensive, but let's assume that you are not going to take lessons right now. A third source of tennis expense is clothes and equipment, and these items will be discussed later in this chapter.

In addition to the possibility of having to make a financial commitment, you will have to make a commitment in terms of time if you want to improve your skills and maintain your level of competency. You cannot play tennis occasionally and expect to do very well. The weekend player has trouble maintaining the strokes and physical condition he or she has achieved. Most adult players do have to settle for that kind of weekend commitment; but those people who really do something with their games play more than twice a week. If you do not have control over how much you get to practice and play, be realistic in your expectations of how good a player you can become.

How Good Can You Become?

There is a difference between people who play tennis and tennis players. People who play tennis are those who occasionally get the rackets out of the closet or garage, find some old balls, and go out to hit them around the court for a while. Their tennis-playing activity is spontaneous and is considered something to do when there is nothing else to do. That's okay. We need those types. They don't tie up the courts very long, anyway. Tennis players, on the other hand, play regularly and they consider tennis to be their primary outlet for recreation, exercise, and social contacts. A person does not have to be good to be considered a tennis player, he just has to place a higher priority on tennis-related activity than on other forms of recreation. For our discussion here of how good any person can become at the game, we will consider only tennis players, not the people who occasionally play tennis.

The person who decides to become a tennis player naturally wants to become the best possible player, given his or her capabilities. How good you can become depends on many factors, such as how old you are, how old you were when you began playing, what your athletic ability is, how much time you have to practice and play, and how interested you are in developing your tennis skills. When these and other factors are combined, you will fall into a rather specific category of tennis player. This category will usually be established a few years after you begin to play. While there are disagreements about how many levels of the game exist, there is seldom a disagreement about which level you fit into at the local, state, or national level. You will know how good you are, your friends will know, and upward or downward mobility into different levels of competition will be difficult. To put it bluntly, after you have reached your level of competence, you will be too good to play with some players and not good enough to play with others.

There are several standardized methods for rating players according to skill. One method, the Si-System, requires that the players rate themselves from "1" to "10" (beginner to world class). The Si-System Ratings, given below, will be referred to throughout this chapter.

SI-SYSTEM RATINGS [1]

Rating	Examples
10	The elite players, the best in the world
9	Top-ranked national amateur players
8	Top-ranked sectional players
7	Top-ranked state or local players
6	Better players who would do well in local "Class A" or citywide tournaments
5	Good club players who would do well in local "Class B" tournaments or country club events
4	Experienced or better than average players
3	Average players who can keep the ball in play
2	Advanced beginners who either have had a few lessons or have been playing less than one year
1	Beginners

Whether you rate yourself informally or use one of the standardized tests, the point is that there are far more classifications of players than beginning, intermediate, and advanced. Within each of those categories there are subdivisions, and each person should set realistic goals regarding how good he or she can become. Although virtually every player can advance beyond the beginner stages to some intermediate stage, relatively few people go on to become advanced players. Of course, you can enjoy the game even if you are not in the top classifications; however, you will enjoy it more if you play with those players who are about as good as you are. Enjoyment also comes from the challenge of trying to reach a higher level of tennis competency.

Let's look at some hypothetical examples and attempt to make some general predictions about how good various players can become. Perhaps you can get a better perspective on levels of ability and be able to establish your own goals by comparing your situation with the ones described here. With a few exceptions, the only players who become world class players (Number 10 in the Si-System Ratings) are those who started playing before they were ten or twelve years old, who received professional instruction during their childhood and adolescent years, who have

[1] © Si Surowski, 1974.

superior athletic ability, who have time to practice and play several hours a day at least five days a week most of the year, and who have an intense competitive drive. That should rule out a few of you. If that same person had decided to wait until age fifteen to twenty before beginning to play, his or her potential would probably be reduced to becoming a top-ranked state or regional player. If the individual with a lot of ability and a lot of time to develop that ability waits until age twenty to thirty to begin playing, that person's potential will probably drop another notch to a "6," a good player who would do well in local tournaments.

Now consider the adult who decides to take up tennis between age twenty and forty, who has average athletic ability, and who has limited time in which to learn and practice the game. This player can become good enough to enjoy participating in local tournaments. The chances of becoming a consistent tournament winner outside of the immediate club or city are not good. This person can certainly become proficient enough to play a respectable game of tennis, to enjoy playing, and to see his or her game improve. This group of players probably accounts for most of those people responsible for the tennis boom of the 1970s.

The person with average ability and a limited amount of time who starts playing later in middle age should realistically settle for fun and gradual improvement. Face the fact that if you are a middle-aged beginner, your game is going to have some severe weaknesses. This is not meant to discourage you from becoming interested in the game. There are enough values in tennis other than becoming a champion to make the game worth playing. There is a huge group of people of all ages who just like to go out and hit or play for the fun of it. These people could not care less about ratings, age divisions, tournaments, and competition. They probably get more enjoyment from tennis than any other group of players.

Try to resist the temptation to assume automatically that you can achieve great heights in competitive tennis. Perhaps you are one of the few who can overcome obstacles of age, limited time, and no instruction, and become a champion player. But you will have more fun and be less frustrated if you play as well as you can, learn as fast as your mind, body, and schedule will allow, and accept the results. If you turn out to be the average weekend tennis player, you will not be disappointed. If you become a great player, consider it a bonus and enjoy the game even more.

Where Can You Play?

The first place to look and the cheapest place to play is at your local public courts. Public courts are those constructed, maintained, and sometimes supervised by some governmental body such as a city or county recreation department. If you are not sure where your public courts are, call the municipal recreation department nearest you and ask. There are thousands of these kinds of courts throughout the country.

Try to find courts that are supervised, if possible. If there is someone in charge, you will have a better chance of getting a court without having to wait very long. Reservations may be necessary. Such courts will probably be in good condition because someone is there to guard against vandalism and to report maintenance problems. You may have to pay for the use of these courts because the supervisors have to be paid. However, the court fees are usually very inexpensive—as little as fifty cents an hour in some places. Another advantage of playing at supervised public courts is that you have a better chance of getting a match if you do not already have one arranged. The person in charge knows the players who come to the tennis center and frequently serves as a tennis matchmaker.

On courts where no one is in charge of the program or court schedule, you do not have to worry about playing time limits or reservations, but you have no guarantee of a reasonably short wait for a court to become available. Neighborhood public courts are often filled with neighborhood youngsters. Unsupervised public courts may have pay-as-you-play lighting systems for night play. Again, the charge is nominal in most places.

A second place to look for an empty court is at schools and colleges. Some secondary schools and most college campuses have tennis courts. These are usually maintained very well, but almost all of them are open to students, faculty, and staff members first, and to the public when those groups are not using them. Few of the courts are supervised, so if you can find out when they are in use by the schools, you may be able to arrange your schedule to avoid a conflict. School courts may be more available to the public during holidays and semester breaks, time periods which could add up to as much as two or three months a year.

The third place to play is at country clubs, racket clubs, and courts owned by institutions such as the YMCA, YWCA, churches, or camps. You must be a member to play on these courts or must be invited by a member, so it is going to cost somebody money. If you are serious about wanting to play and if public court space is limited where you live, the cost of membership may be well worth it. Reservations must be made to play, but the courts will be in excellent condition and playing conditions will be better than anywhere else. There are also excellent auxiliary facilities at many clubs such as pro shops, locker rooms, snack bars, and swimming pools.

Who Can You Play?

With millions of tennis players in the country, finding someone to play with should not be difficult, but sometimes it is. This is especially true for the beginner who is not good enough to play with intermediates and hesitant about asking others to play.

If you are just beginning, look for friends who will play with you. You may be able to make learning a joint adventure with your husband or wife, with a friend, or with a group of friends. It is important to have a group of people who are about as good as you are to play with. You can progress together as you learn and also ensure that you always have someone with whom to play. However, you also need at least one person who is better than you who will occasionally hit with you so that you may improve your game. This presents a delicate situation, because someone who is better than you probably does not want to spend his or her already limited tennis time trying to keep the ball in play for your benefit. To complicate the problem, one of tennis's unwritten rules is that the better player invites the lesser player to hit or play.

Even though this situation requires a sense of diplomacy, it can be handled. If you are a beginner, do not ask the same better player to play with you frequently. Break the unwritten rule and ask a good player who is also a good friend to play with you about once a month. Once a month is enough, especially if that person gets to play tennis only once or twice a week. If your friend plays several times a week, you might get away with asking him or her to play more often than once a month. If you are fortunate enough to have several friends who are good tennis players, try to tap each one once a month. By scheduling them in rotation, you get to play against someone better than you about once a week, which leaves the rest of the week to play with friends on your own level. If you are the better player in the situation just described, you must learn to say "no" to some requests for matches against inferior players, but remember that you were once where they are and that there are players better than you who do not particularly look forward to your requests for matches.

You may also find somebody to play by free-lancing, that is, by just going to local public courts and looking for someone who needs an opponent or a partner. (Do not go to a club where you are not a member to look for a match.) You may have to sit and wait a long time, but at courts with moderate traffic, there will usually be somebody who is also looking for a match. People often show up early or late for matches, some people do not show up at all, and others have to leave before their friends are ready to quit. Any of these circumstances creates an open spot which you can fill. If you are successful at free-lancing, you will meet new friends and playing companions, and you will not have to free-lance as much in the future. If there is somebody in charge of the courts, let that person know you are looking for a match so he can line you up with other unattached players.

Organized competition provides another opportunity for you to meet and compete with people of similar ability. Well-organized municipal, club, and school programs offer various kinds of short-term and continuing competition. Single elimination tournaments are the most frequently used form of tennis competition; these events are usually completed within a period of a few days and they are most often held during the summer months. Tennis leagues are constantly being organized for club members, industrial employees, apartment residents, and participants in city recreation programs. Clubs and city programs also arrange tennis ladders which enable participants to challenge players above them on the ladder. This type of competition is continuing and provides an excellent opportunity for players of any level to have a constant supply of opponents. Find out where the list or ladder is and what the rules are, and put your name at the bottom. If you begin at the bottom, it will be up to you to seek competition; if you are in the middle of the ladder, you can challenge or be challenged to a match. Do not sign up to participate in a tennis ladder unless you know you will be available to play within a reasonable amount of time when someone challenges you.

Which Organizations Can You Join?

If you are very serious about becoming involved in tennis, there are national, regional, and local tennis organizations which you can join. At the national level, the United States Tennis Association is the largest and most prominent organization. The U.S.T.A. is open to any person interested in the game of tennis. Players, officials, and supporters constitute the membership. The organization is involved in a variety of activities, including sanctioning tournaments, conducting junior development programs, supporting Wightman and Davis Cup teams, ranking players, and holding clinics and seminars for players, teachers, and coaches.

The U.S.T.A.'s main office is in New York, and there are seventeen sections throughout the United States. Officials in each of the sections promote and govern tournament competition in their areas. Where a section encompasses more than one state, there may be state U.S.T.A. groups, also. The U.S.T.A. maintains a tennis publications office and a research and education center in New Jersey. Regional tennis film libraries have recently been established across the country.

If you join the United States Tennis Association, you must pay annual dues. For your money you will receive a membership card, will be entitled to participate in sanctioned tournaments, will have the opportunity to be ranked at the state, sectional, or national levels, and will receive some of the organization's publications. Adult members receive the monthly magazine *Tennis U.S.A.*, the official U.S.T.A. publication. Members also receive a sectional yearbook which contains rankings, names of officers and committee members, tournament regulations, and the schedule of tournaments. Some sectional and state associations may provide members with additional publications.

If you are interested in joining the U.S.T.A. write to:

United States Tennis Association
51 East 42nd Street
New York, New York 10017

At the local level, tennis associations have become very popular in the past few years. These organizations may or may not be associated with the U.S.T.A. Where they exist, they are usually composed of tennis-minded people in a community who want a more structured system of competition, instruction, and social activity with other tennis players. These groups may form tennis leagues, sponsor tournaments, hold clinics, and have parties for players. The cost of joining local tennis associations is insignificant, and there is a great opportunity to meet and play tennis with new friends. If there is no such association in your community, you may want to organize one yourself.

If you decide to form your own local tennis association, here are some guidelines to follow:

1.   Get together with a small group of people (less than ten) who share your opinion that a tennis organization is needed. At least one member of the group should have some administrative experience in the game. The other members should be leaders in the tennis community and they should be people who are willing to work.

2.   At the first meeting try to agree on the general goals your organization wants to achieve. Are you organizing so that there will be more competition? Do you want an emphasis on instruction? Is the group for all ages? Is it strictly a tennis-playing association, or will there be social functions?

3.   If you can get general agreement on the purpose of the organization, then try to zero in on one or two immediate projects. Do not try to do too much at the beginning. If the association is successful, there will be plenty of time to expand its services.

4.   Get a commitment from the people present at the first meeting that they will give their time to the association. These organizations frequently fail when everyone wants to play tennis and have a good time, but all of the work is left to two or three people.

5.   Set a time and place, then call a general meeting for anyone in the area who might be interested in joining the group. Publicize the meeting through newspapers, radio and television stations, posters, and telephone calls. At the meeting, the persons should be told what the purposes of the organization are, what kind of activities are being contemplated, and how much it will cost to participate in the association's activities. The cost can be in the form of annual membership dues or on an event-by-event basis. Give everyone a chance to ask questions, then allow people to sign up either as a member of the group or as a participant in the first event. Make it clear that whether or not the association materializes depends on public response and that a decision will be made on future activities after the first meeting or event.

6.   After the first general meeting, the steering committee may want to meet again to make firm decisions on whether or not to pursue the project. If a decision to continue is made, plan the first event and see that it is completed. Then a second meeting may be necessary to elect officers, give awards, or plan other activities.

BUYING EQUIPMENT AND CLOTHES

Rackets

You might already have an old tennis racket with which to get started, or you may be able to borrow an extra racket from a friend. If you have to buy a racket, do not spend a lot of money for one until you have decided to play tennis regularly for a long time. New rackets range in price from five dollars to more than a hundred dollars. Although it is possible to get a racket for less than ten dollars, you should not expect much in quality or durability at that price. In the ten to twenty dollar range, you should be able to find a racket that is adequate for getting started. Most of the major sporting goods companies sell rackets within the entire price range, so the brand name is not that important for a beginner. As you improve your game, you will be able to decide on a racket with a feel that suits you. Before buying an expensive one, try to borrow different rackets from players you know so you can see how each one hits. Picking up and swinging a racket in a store or pro shop is not sufficient to get a racket's feel. The only way to do that is to hit with one.

There are ways to determine if you are getting a quality racket. One way is to look on the throat (the part between the strings and the grip) for markings indicating the racket's grip size and weight. On quality rackets, you will see something like 4½ L, 4⅝ M, 4¾ H, or similar indications (see Figure 1). The numbers refer to the circumference of the grip (handle) in inches and the letter means either a light, medium, or heavyweight racket. If there are no markings, you are looking at a cheap racket. However, there are some inferior rackets with these markings, so this is not the only method of determining the quality of a racket.

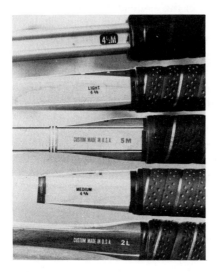

Figure 1. Look for markings on the side of the racket which indicate the size of the grip and weight of the racket.

A second way to judge the quality of some wooden rackets is to look for separate laminated wood strips that form the racket head (the part of the racket where the strings are). Generally, good rackets will have five to twelve strips of wood pressed together at the top. On some good rackets the laminations may not be visible because of the outer finish. Cheaper rackets have fewer wood strips or a one-piece top.

A third method of determining racket quality is to observe the general workmanship of the racket. Does it look cheap or is it well designed? Is the material used to make the grip thick, durable looking leather? Are the laminated strips put together smoothly on a wooden racket? On metal rackets, is the welding or riveting secure?

Finally, it is a good idea to get advice from tennis players and to observe which rackets are being used in your area. Experienced players have probably played with a variety of rackets and they can give you sound advice on what might be best for you. The most popular rackets are frequently the best rackets, so if you see a lot of people playing with a particular brand, it is probably a racket of quality.

You will have to decide whether to buy a racket made of wood or metal. There are many differences between the two kinds, but wooden rackets usually have stiffer frames and give the player more control and less power, whereas metal rackets provide more power but less control. There is a wide range of racket flexibility within each of these two categories, so again it is best if you test various rackets before making a choice. There are also fiberglass rackets on the market; these are somewhere between wood and metal in terms of whippiness or flexibility. Since accuracy will be a problem during the first few months of play, it is probably best to begin playing with a wooden racket. After you have played for a while, you may decide to buy a more expensive racket. Then you can make a final decision regarding steel, aluminum, or fiberglass.

Two other decisions you will have to make before buying a racket involve the size of the grip and the weight of the racket. Grip sizes range from 4 to 5 inches. The most common size for men is 4⅝ inches; women tend to use rackets with slightly smaller grips. If the grip size is too small or too large, the racket may turn in your hand when you hit. The way to determine the proper grip size for you is to shake hands with the racket handle. The lower part of your hand should touch the bottom of the racket handle. As your fingers curl around the grip, the end of the thumb should touch the first joint of the middle finger, as shown in Figure 2. If the thumb does not reach that point, the grip is too large for your hand (Figure 3). If the thumb overlaps the joint, the grip is too small (Figure 4). The shape of the grip should not be overlooked. It is important that you choose a racket that fits the contour of your hand when held tightly. Also remember that racket grips can be replaced and that many handles can be reduced or increased in circumference.

Strung tennis rackets vary in weight from 11 to 15 ounces. The light, medium, and heavy designations mentioned earlier may vary from brand to brand, but lightweight rackets usually weigh less than 13½ ounces, heavy rackets over 14 ounces, and mediums in between. The light rackets are easier to handle, but supply less power; the heavy ones enable you to hit with more force, but added weight may tire your arm out before a match is over. The medium-weight rackets are sold most often to adults and are a compromise between potential power and handling ease. Rackets for children should be on the light side, with smaller than average grip sizes. Rackets a few inches shorter than standard sizes are also available and are effective for children and some adults just starting to play.

Cheap rackets will last less than a year if you play regularly. Quality rackets should last several years if you take care of them. If a racket breaks shortly after you have purchased it, take it back to the dealer and ask for a replacement. Do not waste money buying a racket press. Good rackets should not warp, and bad ones will, presses or no presses. Racket covers are more attractive and useful than presses. Covers protect frames and strings from moisture, and they can be used to hold keys, wallets, and coin purses while you play. They also help you identify your rackets.

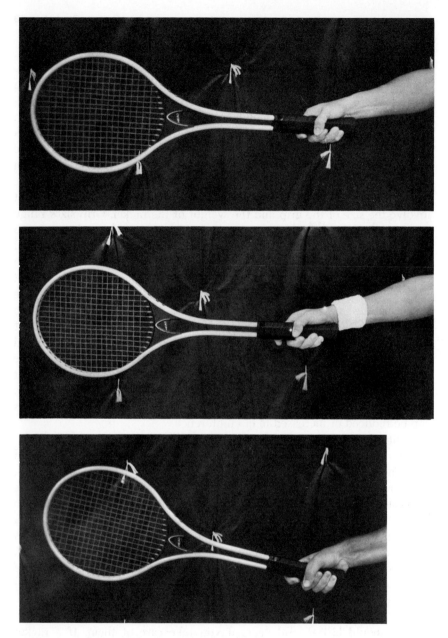

Figure 2 (top). The end of the thumb meets the first joint of the middle finger, indicating that this grip is about the right size.

Figure 3 (center). This player's thumb does not quite reach the first joint of the middle finger. The grip is a little too large.

Figure 4 (bottom). When the thumb overlaps the first joint of the middle finger, the grip may be too small.

14

Beginners need only one racket; intermediates and advanced players frequently own two or more rackets so they will have an alternate if the strings in one break during play or if the grip on one becomes too slick because of moisture.

Strings

Department stores and many sporting goods stores sell rackets already strung. Pro shops more often sell unstrung frames and give you the choice of the kind of strings to be used. Beginners should ask for nylon strings because they are cheap, are reasonably durable, and can be replaced with more expensive strings when the player improves. There are several kinds of nylon strings and many brands. Many advanced players use rackets strung with material other than gut. Gut is a non-euphemism for the beef muscle tissue used as racket string. It is expensive and must be kept dry, but it is an extremely resilient and sensitive stringing material. If money is not a consideration, use gut; if you do not want to pay fifteen to twenty dollars for each restringing job, use nylon strings.

Rackets can be strung from pressure in the 40-pound range to more than 60 pounds. A reasonable average is 51 to 55 pounds. Beginners should have their rackets strung at about 50 to 52 pounds for effective ball control. Local advanced players prefer the 54 to 56 range, and world class players may have their rackets strung at 60 pounds or above.

It is difficult to predict how long racket strings will last. Many beginners and intermediates can play for months with the same set of strings. Advanced players may wear out or break strings in a matter of weeks or even days. Their durability depends on the quality of string, how often you play, your style of game, and how well you take care of your racket. There are commercial products available that may be applied to racket strings to make them last longer.

Balls

Tennis balls come in almost as many varieties as tennis rackets. Here you cannot afford to start out with cheap ones and then graduate to better quality balls as you improve; it is important always to play with good balls, so buy the best ones available the first time out. Brand names can be deceiving, but Dunlop, Penn, Slazenger, Spalding, and Wilson are some of the companies that make good tennis balls. Balls cost from two to four dollars for a can of three. You can save money by watching for sales, shopping at discount stores, or buying a dozen balls at a time.

The balls packaged in cans are packed under pressure. When you open the can, you should hear a hissing sound, which is the pressurized air being released. If you do not hear that sound, return the can to the dealer for a refund or a new can of balls. If a ball breaks within the first two or three sets, all three balls should be returned for a replacement can.

Do not plan to play with one can of balls forever. Three balls may last two or three outings for beginners and some intermediates, but after that either they will begin to lose pressure and bounce, or the fuzz will wear off. When that happens, use them for practice only. You can extend the life of practice balls by putting them through a washing machine and drier. The balls will come out cleaner, lighter, and fluffier than before.

Some tennis balls (Tretorns, for example) are not packaged under pressure. They are sold in a box. These balls are not as bouncy as those that are pressurized, but they never go dead. They will ultimately lose their fuzz and that will affect the bounce of the ball.

Clothes

The tennis clothes game can be expensive unless you are careful. Tennis players have been brainwashed on the subject of appropriate clothing for play. If a group of people go to a gymnasium to play an informal game of basketball, they will probably wear comfortable, informal athletic wear. If those same people play in a city, school, or church league game, they will probably wear some kind of basketball uniform. Tennis players, however, have been taught to think that they should wear "tennis clothes" even for informal play with friends. Why not dress comfortably, informally, and inexpensively for those matches, saving the more formal tennis attire for organized competitive events? The matter should at least be a personal decision, but many clubs require a certain standard of dress for their members. If there is not a written rule regarding clothes, there is certainly a great deal of social pressure on the player who dresses down for informal play. If you play at a club that is clothes conscious, tennis outfits may be more appropriate. For playing in public courts, just about anything that is comfortable is acceptable.

The price for most women's tennis outfits ranges from twenty to fifty dollars. If you sew, you can make your own dresses for ten dollars or less. Men's tennis shorts cost from eight to twenty-five dollars, and shirts sell for five to fifteen dollars. White has been the traditional tennis color, but other colors have been "in" for the past few years. The lighter colors are cooler in hot weather, which is probably why white outfits were popular in the first place. Warmup suits are necessary if you play throughout the year. They vary in style, color, and price just as other tennis items do.

Shoes

In choosing tennis shoes, the four factors to consider are cost, durability, comfort, and weight. Tennis shoes range from five to thirty dollars a pair. Frequency of play, style of play, and the type of court surface will determine how much wear you will get from your shoes. People who play often on hard surfaces may wear out a pair of shoes within a few weeks. Those who play on softer surfaces may get several months out of their shoes. It is not unusual for the toe of one shoe to wear out completely while the rest of the shoe is still in perfect condition. Single shoes are available from some companies. Leather-topped tennis shoes are more comfortable and more expensive than canvas-topped shoes, but if you tend to wear out the sole or toe quickly, the comfort may not be worth the expense.

Buy the lightest shoe possible if you are satisfied with the cost, comfort, and durability factors. A difference of a few ounces may not seem important in the shoe store, but those ounces will seem like pounds during the third set of a match.[2]

WRITTEN AND UNWRITTEN RULES

Rule books for tennis and other sports are written in technical language that may be difficult to understand. These books are seldom indexed, making it even more difficult for the reader to find the answer to a specific question. Instead of rewriting the rules of tennis here, the most frequently asked questions about the rules will be answered. Some of the questions will seem simple to the intermediate and advanced players, but those questions are perfectly reasonable and proper to the beginning player. Therefore, all questions, simple and complicated, will be given equal attention. In addition to giving answers to questions about clearly defined tennis rules, the answers will also include comments about some of the unwritten rules of the game. For another author's views on the unwritten rules of tennis, read *The Code* by Nick Powell. *The Code* contains a thorough discussion of various situations not covered by the rules. It is available in booklet form, has been adopted by several official tennis organizations, and is distributed by the United States Tennis Association publications center.

[2] Jim and Arlene Brown, "A Woman's Guide to Beginning Tennis," *The Woman*, 10, no. 6 (June 1975), 110–15.

1. *How do you keep score?* The server's score is always given first. Points are as follows: love: 0; first point won by either player: 15; second point: 30; third point: 40; fourth point: game. If both players are tied at four or more points during a game, the score is called "deuce." When one player goes ahead by one point after the score is deuce, the score is called "ad in" if the server is ahead and "ad out" if the receiver is ahead. A player must win two consecutive points after the score is deuce in order to win that game.

2. *What is a set?* A set has been completed when one player or team has won at least six games and is ahead by at least two games (6-0, 6-1, 6-2, 6-3, or 6-4). If a player wins at least six games but is not ahead by at least two games, the set continues until one player is ahead by two games (7-5, 8-6, 9-7, etc.). This procedure is followed unless a tie breaker is used to complete a set.

3. *What is a tie breaker?* A tie breaker is commonly used to complete a set when the score is 6-6 in games. Instead of playing until one player gains a two-game lead, the players play a series of points, the winner of which wins that set. The most popular tie breaker consists of the best of nine points. The player (Smith) whose turn it is to serve serves a point from the right side of the court and then serves a point from the left side. Then his opponent (Jones) serves the next two points, first from the right and then from the left side. The players then change ends of the court and the first server (Smith) serves two more points. If neither player has won five points, the serve goes back to the second player (Jones), who serves the last three points. On the ninth point of a tie breaker, the receiver (Smith) has the choice of receiving the serve from either the left or right side of the court. The winner of the tie breaker wins the set, 7-6.

4. *What is the order of serves when a tie breaker is necessary in doubles?* Teams use the order of serves just described for singles play. In doubles, the players on both teams serve from the sides established during the preceding set.

5. *How does the next set after a tie breaker begin?* The players stay on the ends of the court where the tie breaker was completed. The player or team who served second in the tie breaker serves the first game of the next set. The players play one game, then change ends of the court.

6. *What is a match?* A match is whatever the tournament director says it is in formal competition or whatever two or four players decide it is in informal competition. A match usually consists of two out of three sets, but it can be three out of five sets or a pro set. A match may also refer to competition between two tennis teams.

7. *What is a pro set?* A pro set has been completed when one player wins at least eight games and is ahead by at least two games (8-0, 8-1, 8-2, etc.).

8. *Who keeps score?* In some tournament competition, there may be an umpire assigned to a match, and he will call out the score. In most cases, however, the players keep their own score, and the server should call out the score before each point is played.

9. *How is a point won?* Most often a player wins a point when his or her opponent does not serve or return a ball over the net and into the proper court.

10. *Are balls that hit the lines good?* Yes.

11. *Are balls that hit the top of the net in play?* Serves that hit the top of the net and fall into the proper court are repeated without any penalty. This is called a "let." Other shots that hit the top of the net and fall into the proper court are in play.

12. *Where do you stand if you are the server?* To begin the first point of a game, stand behind the baseline and to the right of the center mark. On the second point, move to the left side of the center mark as you face the net. Alternate serving from the right and left sides on each point for the rest of the game. Remember that the same person serves the entire game. In doubles, the rule is the same except that you can stand as far out behind the baseline as the alley.

13. *How many times can the server have to put the ball into play?* Two chances on each point, not counting lets.

14. *How many times can the server serve a let on the same point?* There is no limit.

15. *What is a foot fault?* A foot fault is committed when the server touches the court on or beyond the baseline before striking the ball. The player who commits a foot fault loses that chance to serve the ball into play.

16. *Who calls foot faults?* In tournaments where there are linespersons, they call the violations. In informal competition, the rule is seldom enforced. You are on your honor not to foot fault and you should politely complain to your opponent if you know he or she is foot faulting. Be sure that you are not guilty before complaining about someone else.

17. *When do players change ends of the court?* When the total number of games in a set equals an odd number.

18. *Who calls shots in or out?* If there are no linespersons, each player is responsible for calling shots out on his side of the court. If the shot is in, do not say anything. If the shot is out, shout "out" whether or not you swing at or hit the ball.

19. *What if you are not sure whether a ball was in or out?* If the shot was that close, you should play the ball as if it were in. If the shot was the last in a rally and you are not sure, ask for your opponent's opinion. If he or she says it was out, it was out. If he or she says it was in, it was in. If your opponent does not know, it is your call and you should give the other player the benefit of the doubt.

20. *What if you think your opponent is cheating you?* Complain to him or her. If that does not work, stop the match and ask for an umpire.

21. *Can a player reach over the net to hit a ball?* Not unless the ball has bounced on that player's side of the net and is carried back across the net by the wind or spin.

22. *Can a player touch the net?* Not while the point is in progress.

23. *Does the ball have to clear the top of the net?* No, a ball can be returned around the sides of the net posts.

24. *How do you determine who serves first?* Spin a racket or flip a coin. The winner of the spin may choose to serve the first game, to receive the serve in the first game, or begin play on either side. The loser of the spin gets to choose either the side or the order of serve, depending on what the winner decided to do.

25. *Can you throw your racket at the ball and hit it?* Not legally.

26. *Can you deliberately distract your opponent before or during a point?* No.

27. *In doubles, can partners change sides of the court from which they receive the serve during a set?* No. They can change at the beginning of the next set.

28. *Do doubles partners have to maintain the order of serve during the entire match?* No. The order of serve can be changed at the beginning of each set.

29. *What happens when a ball hits a permanent fixture near the court?* The player who last hit the ball loses the point.

30. *What happens if a player serves from the wrong side of the court?* The point stands, and the players play the next point from the proper court, depending on what the score is.

31. *What happens when doubles partners play a point after having lined up on the wrong sides of their court?* The point stands, and the correction is made at the end of that game.

32. *How high is the net?* Three feet at the center; 3 feet, 6 inches at the net posts.

33. *Can a player serve with an underhand motion?* Yes.

34. *What determines if the receiver is ready to return a serve?* If the receiver attempts to return a serve, he is ready. So if you are not ready, make no attempt to hit the ball. Ask the server to start over.

35. *Can the server toss the ball and catch it rather than serve it?* Yes, but it is a fault if he swings and misses.

36. *What happens if you are standing outside the boundary line and a ball that would have been out touches you first?* The player who catches or touches the ball loses the point.

37. *How much time is a player allowed between games when players change ends of the court?* A maximum of one minute.

38. *How much time should a player be allowed between matches in a tournament?* At least fifteen minutes.

39. *How much time should a player be allowed after the announced starting time of a match before a forfeit is declared?* Each tournament director establishes the rules regarding defaults, but fifteen minutes is usually the maximum time allowed.

40. *How much time is allowed if a player cannot continue to play because of an injury?* If the injury is a temporary one caused by an accident, such as running into a fence or falling on the court, the umpire should give that player a reasonable amount of time to recover (a few seconds, or at most, a couple of minutes). If the player cannot continue because of "natural loss of physical condition," such as cramps or illness, no time for recovery is allowed.

41. *What happens if a ball rolls onto your court while a point is in progress?* A let is in order if either player calls for a let before the point is completed. In this case, playing a let means replaying the point entirely. This does not mean that you or the other player should delay the call until you see that you may lose the point. Before returning the ball to the proper court, make sure that returning it will not interrupt a point in progress.

42. *What happens if a ball in play strikes a ball lying on the court?* The player or team on whose side the ball is lying loses the point.

43. *Can a player touch the ball with any part of his body during a point?* No.

44. *In doubles, does the server's partner have to stand at the net while the serve is being delivered?* No, the partner can stand anywhere he or she wants to.

45. *Can a coach talk with a player for the purpose of giving instructions during a match?* Most conferences, leagues, and tournaments have their own rules regarding coaching during a match. The U.S.T.A. has ruled that it is not permissible unless a local rule has been made.

46. *Who is the final authority in a tournament match?* The umpire.

47. *Is there any rest period in a two out of three set match?* In men's competition, no; in women's there may be a ten-minute rest period after the second set.

48. *In a match without linespersons, can the receiver's partner call a serve out?* Yes.

49. *Should a point be replayed if the ball breaks during the point?* Yes.

50. *If a match is delayed by rain, are the players allowed a warmup period when play resumes?* Yes.

SPEAKING THE LANGUAGE

If you learn tennis terminology, you will have a better understanding of the game and will be able to communicate more effectively with other players. The following terms and expressions are separated into three groups: scoring and rules, strokes and play, and organization and administration of the game. You may want to refer back to this section as you read the rest of the book.

Scoring and Rules

ad   advantage; refers to the point after the score is deuce
ad court   the left half of a player's court as that player faces the net from the baseline
ad in   a reference to the score when the player serving has won the point after the score was deuce
ad out   a reference to the score when the player receiving the serve has won the point after the score was deuce

all a tie score; for example, "30 all" means that the score is 30-30

alley the 4½ foot wide lanes running parallel to and on both sides of the singles court; the alleys are in play for all shots after the serve in doubles

baseline the boundary line that runs parallel to and 39 feet from the net

carry a shot which is carried on the racket strings, slung, or hit twice as the ball is returned; carries are illegal and may be called by the umpire or the player who hits the shot on which the violation occurs

center mark a line dividing the baseline at the center; the server may not legally step on the center mark before striking the ball

center service line the line in the middle of the court that divides the two service courts

default the awarding of a match to one player because an opponent fails to appear or is not able to complete the match

deuce a tie score at 40-40 and each time thereafter in the same game

deuce court the right half of a player's court as that player faces the net from the baseline

double fault failure on both attempts to serve into the proper court

doubles a match played with four players; also an expression sometimes used to indicate a double fault

fault failure on an attempt to serve into the proper court

forfeit synonym for default

hook a slang term meaning to cheat

let a serve that hits the top of the net and bounces in the proper service court; also an expression used to indicate that a point should be replayed for a number of other reasons

linesperson an official who is responsible for calling balls out at either the baseline, service line, sideline, or center service line

long an informal expression used to indicate that a shot is out

love an archaic, but commonly used word meaning zero in the tennis scoring system

match a contest between two players in singles, four players in doubles, or between two teams, as when two school teams compete against each other

match point the stage of a match when a player can win the match by winning the next point; the term is used by spectators and television commentators during a match and by players after a match; it is not used by the umpire or players in calling out the score

mixed doubles competition between a man and woman on one team against a man and woman on the other team

net umpire an official who is responsible for calling let serves

no an expression which some players use to call a shot out

no-ad   a relatively new innovation in the scoring system in which a maximum of seven points constitutes a game; if the score is tied at three points for each player, the next player to win a point wins the game

not up   an expression used to indicate that a ball has bounced twice on the same side before being hit

out   a call indicating that a shot has bounced outside a boundary line

pro set   a match which is completed when one player has won at least eight games and is ahead by at least two games

receiver   the player who will return a serve

referee   an official who is responsible for supervising all competition during a tournament

second   an expression used by some players to indicate the first serve was out

serve   the shot used to put the ball into play at the beginning of a point

service break   the loss of a game by the player serving

service court   the area of a court into which the ball must be served; its boundaries are the net, the center line, the service line, and the singles sideline; the server tries to serve into the service court diagonally across the net from where he or she stands

service line   the line that runs parallel to and 21 feet from the net

set   that part of a match which is completed when a player has won at least six games and is ahead by at least two games; the set may continue until one player has a two-game advantage, or a tie breaker may be played when each player has won six games

set point   the stage of a set when a player can win the set by winning the next point

sideline   the boundary line that runs from the net to the baseline; the singles sidelines are closer to the center of the court than the doubles sidelines

split   an expression used to indicate that two players or teams have each won a set

sudden death   a tie breaker or the last point of a tie breaker

take two   an expression indicating that the server should repeat both service attempts

tie breaker   method of completing a set when both players or teams have won six games

umpire   a person who is responsible for officiating a specific match between two players or doubles teams

VASSS   Van Alen Simplified Scoring System, in which 21 or 31 points constitute a set

wide   an expression used by some players to indicate a shot was outside of a sideline

Strokes and Play

ace　a serve which the receiver cannot touch with the racket

American twist　a type of serve in which the spin imparted by the racket is the opposite of what it would normally be; a righthander's American twist serve has left-to-right spin on the ball

angle shot　a shot which crosses the net at a severe angle

approach shot　a shot which the hitter follows to the net

Australian doubles　a doubles formation in which the player at net lines up on the same side as the server

back court　that part of the court between the service line and the baseline

backhand　a stroke which a righthanded player hits by reaching across the body to the left side

backspin　reverse spin on the ball, like a car wheel in reverse

backswing　the preparation for a stroke in which the racket is drawn back before being swung forward

big game　a style of play in which emphasis is placed on a hard serve, volleys, and overhead smashes

block　the return of a ball with a very short swinging motion

chip　a groundstroke hit with a short backswing and with backspin on the ball; the chip is directed at the feet of an opponent

choke　to play poorly because of the pressure of competition

choke up　to hold the racket at a point away from the base of the grip

chop　a shot hit with backspin to any part of the court

closed stance　a position in which the toes of both feet form a line parallel with either sideline

Continental grip　a way of holding the racket so that the player does not have to change grips between the forehand and backhand strokes; a more complete description is given in the chapter entitled "Learning the Strokes"

crosscourt　a shot hit diagonally from one corner of the court to the opposite corner

deep　a reference to the area near the baseline

dink　a shot hit with very little pace or depth

down the line　a shot hit parallel to either sideline

drive　a groundstroke hit forcefully and deeply into an opponent's back-court

drop shot　a softly hit shot, usually having backspin, which barely clears the net and bounces within 2 or 3 feet from the net

error　a point lost as a result of one player's mistake rather than the other player's good shot

fast a reference to a tennis court surface on which the ball bounces low and moves rapidly toward the hitter

flat reference to a shot hit with little or no spin

follow through that part of the swinging motion after the ball has been hit

forehand a stroke which a righthanded player hits on the right side of the body

grip the manner in which a racket is held; also, that part of the racket where it is held

groundstroke a shot which is hit after the ball has bounced on the court

hacker a tennis player who does not play the game well

half volley a shot hit just after the ball has bounced on the court; contact is made below the level of the knees

hold serve a game won by the server

lob a high, arching shot

lob volley a lob hit with a volley

no man's land the area of the court between the service line and the baseline; this area is usually considered a poor part of the court from which to attack or defend

overhead smash a hard, powerful stroke hit from an over-the-head racket position

pace the velocity with which the ball is hit

passing shot a reference to a groundstroke hit out of the reach of an opponent at the net

percentage shot the safest, most effective shot hit in a particular situation

placement a winning shot hit to an open area of the court

poach movement of a player at the net in front of his partner to hit a volley

pusher a type of player who is consistent, but who hits with very little pace

rally an exchange of shots

racket head the part of the racket where the strings are attached

ready position the position in which a player stands while waiting for a shot

retriever a type of player, much like the pusher, who gets everything back but does not play aggressively

rush to move toward the net

slice to hit a ball with sidespin, like the spin of a top

slow a reference to a court surface on which the ball bounces and slows down after the bounce

straight sets a reference to winning a match without losing a set

stroke the manner in which a ball is hit

throat   the part of the racket just below the head

topspin   the bottom to top rotation imparted to a ball by a racket, like a car wheel going forward

touch   the ability to hit a variety of precision shots

unforced error   a point lost with absolutely no pressure having been exerted by the opponent

volley   a shot hit before the ball bounces on the court

Organization and Administration

amateur   a person who does not accept money for playing or teaching tennis

Association of Tennis Professionals   an organization composed of most of the leading male tennis players in the world

circuit   a series of tennis tournaments at the state, sectional, national, or international level

closed tournament   an event open only to members of a particular geographical area

Davis Cup   an international team tennis event for male players; a match or "tie" between the teams representing two countries consists of four singles matches and one doubles match

finals   the match played to determine the winner of a tournament

Grand Slam   a reference to a player having won the Australian Open, French Open, United States Open, and Wimbledon in the same year

International Lawn Tennis Federation   an organization which governs international amateur competition and which has some jurisdiction over professional tennis

invitational tournament   a tournament open only to players who have been invited to participate

junior   a player eighteen years old or younger

junior veteran   a player between 35 and 45 years old

ladder tournament   a type of competition in which the names of participants are placed in a column; players may advance up the column or ladder by challenging and defeating players whose names appear above their own

open tennis   competition open to amateur and professional players

qualifying round   a series of matches played to determine which players will be added to a tournament field

round robin   a type of competition in which all participants compete against all other participants in a series of matches; the player who finishes the competition with the best win-loss percentage is the winner

senior   a player over 45 years of age

single elimination tournament   a type of competition in which players' names are drawn and placed on lines in a tournament bracket; matches are played between players whose names appear on connected bracket lines; players who win advance to the next round of competition; those who lose a match are eliminated

teaching pro   a person who teaches people to play tennis and is paid for his services; teaching pros are usually distinguished from playing pros, although some professionals do both

United States Tennis Association   the organization which governs amateur tennis in the United States

Virginia Slims   a circuit or series of tournaments for female professional tennis players

Wightman Cup   competition for women players representing the United States and England

Wimbledon   a tournament held in England, generally considered to be the most prestigious in the world

World Championship of Tennis   a series of tournaments for male professional players

World Team Tennis   a tennis league composed of male and female professional players who play on teams representing various cities; competition consists of singles, doubles, and mixed doubles

World Tennis Association   an organization consisting of the world's leading female professional players

2

Learning the Strokes

INTRODUCTION

If you are going to learn tennis strokes without taking lessons, there are three problems you must solve. The first problem is to learn how each shot should be hit. While there is room for individuality in executing the various strokes, there are some fundamental principles which you have to know.

The second problem is how to teach yourself these fundamentals. Not only do you have to know what to do, you have to be able to do it. Taking tennis lessons may be the most effective way of learning and practicing the strokes, but it is not the only way. Just as people teach themselves how to play other sports, how to cook, how to build things, and even how to speak foreign languages, so people can and have taught themselves to play tennis.

The third problem is what to do when something goes wrong. Even though you may know the fundamentals and may have taught yourself to play, your game is not necessarily set for life. Learning to play tennis is a continuous process, and whether you have had lessons or not, you should learn how to recognize problems with strokes, how to analyze what is wrong with the strokes, and how to do something to correct the problems.

In this chapter each stroke will be discussed following these three guidelines: how should the shot be hit, how can you teach yourself how to hit it, and what can you do when something goes wrong.

THE SERVE

The Grip

How you hold the racket for the serve depends on how good you are. If you are a beginner, a number one in the Si-System Ratings, your grip will be different than if you are an intermediate or advanced player. This is because the grip used by advanced players is very awkward for people just learning to play. The beginner's grip is comfortable and allows a reasonable amount of control over the ball. As the service motion becomes more fluid, the grip can be changed to accommodate the swing. As you graduate into an advanced service grip, you can hit the ball in a wider variety of ways.

If you are a beginner, put the racket down on the floor or on the court. Reach down and pick up the racket at the bottom of the handle so that your fingers curl around the grip. Your little finger should be about one-half inch from the base of the grip. Extend your arm straight out in front of you and cock your wrist upward. You should be holding the racket and looking directly through the strings as the player in Figure 5 is doing. Take the left edge of the racket and turn it 90 degrees in your hand without moving your wrist or anything else so that you are now looking at the edge of the racket frame head (Figure 6). Next, turn the racket back toward the first position without moving the wrist, but stop halfway between the two positions just described (Figure 7). Adjust your fingers slightly so that you are holding the racket comfortably without changing the angle of the racket. You are now holding the racket with a proper grip for a beginner's serve.

If you are an intermediate level player, follow these same instructions up to the point where you are looking at the edge of the racket frame head (Figure 6). This is the approximate grip for the serve at your level of play, and it is not greatly different from a backhand grip. There may be slight variations to accommodate your particular style, but the basic service grip is the one you are holding now.

Position of the Feet

Stand facing the net with both feet about one inch behind the baseline just to the right of the center mark (Figure 8). Turn 90 degrees to

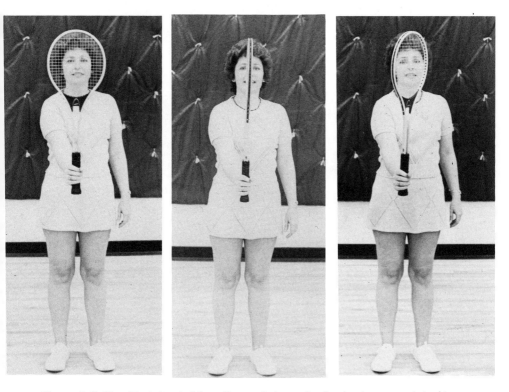

Figure 5 (left). Start by holding the racket up in front of you and looking through the strings.

Figure 6 (center). The second step is to take the left edge of the racket and turn it so that you are looking at the edge of the frame.

Figure 7 (right). Now move the racket back toward the first position, stopping at this position.

your right (if you are a righthander) so that you are looking down the baseline and the outer edge of your left foot is parallel to the baseline (Figure 9). If you are lefthanded, start out facing the net and turn 90 degrees to the left, so that the outer edge of your right foot is parallel to the baseline. Now, whichever way you are facing, move back toward the first position, but stop at a point halfway between the two positions just described. You should be standing at about a 45-degree angle to the net, facing in the direction of the net post (Figure 10). Put your weight on the foot away from the baseline and spread your feet a bit wider than the width of your shoulders. The stance is quite similar to the one most people assume when they stand to carry on an informal conversation. This is a good starting position for beginning and intermediate tennis players. Some teachers allow beginners to face the net squarely while they are learning to serve, and some intermediate and advanced players change the position

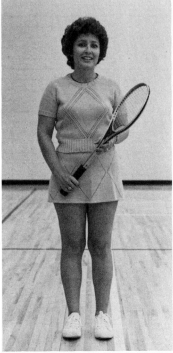

Figure 8 (top left). To find the correct position for your feet, start in this position.

Figure 9 (top right). Now turn 90 degrees to your right.

Figure 10 (left). Finally, turn back toward the first position, stopping when the foot closest to the baseline is at about a 90-degree angle.

of their feet to achieve special effects on their serves. But the 45-degree angle position is comfortable and effective for players at all levels. The position of the feet will change as the weight moves forward during the serve. That will be discussed later.

The Toss

The toss for the serve is the same for all players. Some players may change the toss slightly to execute a particular kind of serve, but the basics are the same. In order to measure the proper height of the toss, hold the racket in one of the service grips described earlier and extend your arm and racket upward as high as you can comfortably reach. Now position the racket head slightly in front of you so that if something were to fall off of the top of the racket, it would fall about 12 inches inside the baseline in front of your feet. With the arm and racket fully extended and slightly in front of you and the baseline, the ball should be tossed so that it reaches a peak in the middle of your racket strings (Figure 11). If that seems rather precise, it should be. If the toss is not where you want it to be, catch the ball or let it drop to the court and start over. You can learn to toss the ball exactly to the right spot every time.

Tossing the ball for the serve involves technique, also. Hold a ball at the base of the fingers of your tossing hand and extend your arm outward in the direction of the net post you are facing (Figure 12). Now lift your arm without bending it very much at the elbow. As you lift your arm, release the ball by extending your fingers. The ball should be tossed without spin. If it comes off of your fingertips, the ball will have spin. If you extend the fingers by spreading them as you toss, the spin should be minimal and the accuracy of your toss increased.

The Swing

If you are a beginner, hold the racket with the beginner's service grip, stand in the position described earlier, and raise the racket up so that the racket head is behind your head. Reach back and scratch your back with the racket (Figure 13). Now raise the racket head again so that it is behind your head and your arm is bent at the elbow at a 90-degree angle (Figure 14). From that starting position, pretend that you are going to throw the racket over the net.

You must be able to throw a ball properly before you can swing a racket in the serving motion correctly. To throw a ball from a starting position behind the head, you must bring forward the shoulder first, following it rapidly but in order by the elbow and finally the hand. Remember that sequence—shoulder, elbow, hand—all brought forward

Figure 12 (above). The server has extended her arm in the direction of the net post prior to the toss.

Figure 11 (left). Practice tossing the ball so that you can toss to a point where your arm and racket are extended up and slightly in front of your body.

smoothly and extending fully at the point where the racket will make contact with the ball on a serve (Figure 15).

Now follow through with the imaginary throwing of the racket across the net. Starting with your arm up and racket up and behind your head, elbow bent, go through with the throwing motion. Reach outward and upward so that your arm fully extends at the point of contact. As you make contact with the ball, the wrist should begin to snap forward in a flexing motion. Follow through by bringing the racket down and across the front of your body, finishing with the racket down by the left leg, if you are righthanded (Figure 16).

If you are an intermediate level player, the swing should be different. It is a full pendulum-like motion, beginning with the racket out in front of the body about chest high (Figure 17). Remembering the ball-

Figure 13 (left). Scratch your back with the racket.

Figure 14 (right). Now raise the racket head and your arm to form two 90-degree angles.

throwing motion, bring the arm and racket down so that the head of the racket passes a point somewhere between the knees and the ankle (Figure 18). As you bring the racket up and behind your back, your arm should begin to bend at the elbow and move through the back-scratching position. From that point on, the motion should be similar to the beginner's motion, with the arm and racket fully extending at the point of contact and following through down and across the body. The racket motion ends low on the opposite side of the body from where swing began (Figure 16).

Putting the Parts Together

Up to this point the serve has been described in its component parts. But the serve itself must be one continuous, smoothly coordinated motion if it is to be effective. If each component is executed separately, the result will be a series of jerky, nonrhythmic movements. As you read the following paragraphs, try to picture yourself serving.

Beginners: Put the ball out in front of your body with the nonracket hand and at the same time position the racket behind your head (Figure

19). As the ball reaches a peak on the toss, bring the racket forward in the throwing motion and hit the ball with your arm and racket fully extended (Figure 20). If you toss the ball well in front of your body, you should have to move your body's weight forward to make contact. The foot closest to the baseline should not move, but the other foot may leave the ground and come forward as you hit and follow through. Your momentum may carry that foot slightly inside the baseline after you make contact (Figure 21); that is a good sign that you are getting a weight transfer into the ball as you serve.

Intermediates: Begin with the racket out in front of your body about chest high and with the nonracket hand holding the ball against the

Figure 15. Everything is extended when you make contact with the ball on the serve.

Figure 16. Follow through down and across your body.

Figure 17 (left). Put the balls on the strings in front of your body.

Figure 18 (right). Let the racket head drop low before you bring your racket up behind your back.

racket strings (Figure 22). As the racket begins to drop into the pendulum motion, the opposite hand should also move slightly downward preliminary to the toss. Both hands move downward at the same time, but the racket arm will be moving down, then into the back-scratching position while the other arm begins to move upward to lift the ball on the toss (Figure 23). The toss has to be timed so that the ball will reach its highest point at the same time the arm and racket extend to make contact. If the timing is not right, stop everything and start again. The toss also has to be far enough in front of the body to force you to lean forward and beyond the baseline as you hit the ball.

At the same time that the racket arm extends for the serve, the position of the feet will change. There are two ways this change can take place. To get your weight into the ball, you have to lean forward. As you lean forward, the foot closest to the baseline stays in the same place, but the other foot must be brought forward. Some players prefer to take one step, starting with the rear foot several inches from the baseline and finishing one step inside the baseline (Figures 24 and 25). Other players

Figure 19. Beginners, start with your racket up and back, and the ball out in front.

Figure 20. Extend your arm upward to hit your serve. Watch the ball until it leaves your racket strings.

Figure 21. Your follow through may carry you one step inside the baseline.

Figure 22 (left). If you are an intermediate, start with the racket and ball in front of the body.

Figure 23 (right). The left arm moves upward for the toss while the right arm moves toward the backscratching position.

make a two-step approach with the rear foot. The server brings the back foot forward and even with the foot closest to the baseline just before the moment of contact with the ball. This movement results in a springboard effect into the service motion and may even give you added height and leverage if you go up on your toes as you hit. After the ball has been served, the foot continues forward, touching down one step inside the baseline (Figure 26).

Regardless of which method you use, try to keep your knees slightly bent during the first part of the service motion. As you hit the ball, the knees and everything else will be extended so that your body forms a straight diagonal line (Figure 27). The action of the knees going from a flexed position to an extended position at the moment of impact will also give a springboard effect to your serve, resulting in added power.

Teaching Yourself How to Serve

Now you know the fundamentals of the serve. The next problem is how to mold the grip, the stance, the toss, the weight transfer, the swing, and the follow through into an actual rhythmic, reliable pattern on the court. Here are some drills, exercises, and learning techniques to help you achieve that goal. Some of these suggestions may be too simple for you if you have been playing for a while; others may be too difficult. Select the ones you enjoy doing and the ones that seem to help you improve the most. There is something here for almost every level of tennis player.

1. *Play catch with someone.* Get a tennis ball, softball, or baseball, and practice throwing back and forth with your wife, husband, children, or friends. Throw for at least ten minutes the first session and try to add to the practice period every day. Stand at least 10 yards from your partner, and work on developing a smooth, loose motion. Remember that

Figure 24 (left).   With the one-step approach, the right foot starts in this position.

Figure 25 (right).   The right foot has moved from a position behind the line to a spot inside the baseline—all in one motion.

the serving motion is like the throwing motion. If you do not feel comfortable, get advice from your throwing partner. As your strength increases and the motion becomes more fluid, increase the throwing distance

Figure 26 (left). In the two-step approach, the right foot is brought forward and is used to push the body forward into the serve.

Figure 27 (right). The body extends into an almost straight diagonal line at the moment of contact with the ball.

until you can easily throw a tennis ball 60 feet. That is the distance from the baseline to the service line on the opposite side of the net. If you cannot throw that far, you are going to have difficulty developing a strong serve.

2. *Throw a tennis ball from the baseline into the proper service court.* Take lots of balls with you to the courts so you will not have to stop to collect the balls after every few throws. It would be even better if you could take a partner with you to catch throws after they have bounced and return them to you.

3. *Practice the service toss by aiming for a target.* Place a basket or a racket cover, or draw a circle at a point inside the baseline where a correct service toss would land if the ball is not hit. See how many times you can execute the toss so that it hits the target.

4. *Serve from the service line.* If you are a beginner, use the technique described earlier and practice serving into the left and right service courts from the service line instead of the baseline. As your accuracy and strength improve, gradually move back toward the baseline.

5. *Serve into the fence surrounding the court or into a wall outside your home.* If you do not have a basket of balls, practice your service motion by serving into the fence so you will not have to waste time chasing balls.

6. *Practice the service motion with the cover on the racket.* The added weight and resistance will help strengthen your serving arm. You can increase the weight further by putting things into the racket cover and placing it on the racket head.

7. *Practice the service motion in front of a mirror.* If you do not have high ceilings where you live, choke up on the racket, use a paddle, or simulate the swing with the palm of your hand. If you know how the serve is supposed to be hit, you can perfect your swing by watching yourself go through the motion.

8. *Serve from a position several feet behind the baseline.* Take three steps back from your normal serving position and serve into the proper court. Now move back as far as you can from the baseline and practice your serve. The practice at long distance will increase your strength and make serving from the baseline much easier.

9. *Count the number of consecutive balls served into each service court.* Try to add to the total each practice session. Set goals of 10, 20, 30, 40, or 50 good serves. Compete with a partner to make practicing more interesting.

10. *Serve while holding the racket several inches from the bottom of the grip.* As your accuracy improves, move your hand gradually down toward the normal position near the base of the grip.

11. *Serve to targets in the service court.* Place a racket cover or tennis ball can in the prime target areas (the corners of the box) and try to hit the objects with your serves.

12. *Play a game with a friend using only the serve and the service return.* Every serve into the proper court earns one point. Every return of serve into the singles court also earns a point. Each point ends after the serve or after the serve and a return. The server gets two chances to get the serve into play.

Recognizing and Solving Your Own Problems With the Serve

You are ready for the third and most frustrating of the three problems you have in teaching yourself to play tennis. Even though you may have a fundamental knowledge of the serve and even though you may have practiced it for some time, you are going to have problems with it. Even the great players of the world develop problems with the serve and with every other stroke. The problems and solutions are usually about the same for all players, whether beginners or pros. If you can learn to spot the symptoms of a poor serve, you may be able to correct your own mistakes. If you can do this, you will have a significant advantage over other tennis players. Here are some problem areas with this stroke, possible causes, and suggestions for corrections.

1. *Lack of power.* Insufficient power might simply be caused by a lack of strength. If you are weak in the upper body and in the arms, you are probably going to have a weak serve. Learn to live with this problem unless you are willing to exercise, lift weights, or perform isometrics to increase your muscular fitness. Specific suggestions for conditioning and strength building will be presented in another section.

Another possible cause for a weak serve is not getting the full weight of the body into the ball. Many beginning and intermediate players use only their arms, which is tiring as well as ineffective. To use the whole body in the serve, the weight must be moved forward. One of the most common causes for failure to move forward is a toss that is above or behind the head instead of in front of it.

A third possibility might be the lack of wrist action as the ball is hit. "Wrist action" is a more appropriate description of what should happen than "wrist snap," which is the term most teachers and writers use.

Actually, the wrist does not snap or flex until after the ball has been hit, so snapping the wrist will not increase the power of the serve. The inward rotation of the thumb, called "pronation," is responsible for the whiplike motion that gives added force to the serve. So as you serve, concentrate on rapidly rotating the thumb inward just as you make contact with the ball.

Lack of power could also be caused by little or no follow through. If you stop the racket at the point of contact with the ball, your serve will be more of a punch than a full stroke.

Finally, failure to bend the knees and spring out toward the ball can cause you to serve without much power. Do not be stiff-legged.

2. *Hitting the ball consistently beyond the service court.* The most obvious cause of this problem is hitting the ball too hard. Remember that two three-quarter speed serves are much more effective than hitting the first serve very hard and hitting the second serve very softly. If you always seem to be hitting deep, try to hit with less force.

Hitting beyond the service court may also result when the angle of the racket is out of line with where you want the ball to go. If the racket face is tilted too far upward, the ball is naturally going to reflect off the strings and sail out. Every player must be conscious of the angle at which the ball strikes the racket. Keep your eyes on the ball as long as possible while you are serving. You may be able to observe the angle at which you are hitting.

3. *Hitting the ball consistently wide to either side of the service court.* Check your grip. A beginner who holds the racket too far toward the backhand grip on the serve may slice the ball too much, thus pulling the ball to the left side (if the player is righthanded). If that is the problem, go back to the beginner's grip described earlier.

If the problem persists, try rotating the wrist to adjust the racket head to the right angle at the moment of contact. If you are righthanded and the ball goes too far to the left, rotate your wrist outward slightly just before you hit the ball. If your serves are going to the right of the service court, concentrate on bringing the wrist and arm down and across the front of your body as you hit.

4. *Hitting into the net.* Check the height of your toss. You may be tossing too low, hurrying your swing, and slapping down at the ball. Also check your concentration. If you are consistently serving the ball into the bottom of the net, you may not be paying close enough attention to your business. Pick out a spot deep in the service court and try to hit that spot.

5. *Loss of balance.* Be sure your feet are aligned properly prior to the serve. If that seems okay, make sure your toss is where you want it to

be. Sometimes players toss erratically and instead of restarting the serving motion, they go ahead and chase the toss wherever it leads them.

6. *General inconsistency.* Examine the component parts of your serve one by one. Start with the grip, then go through each phase—stance, toss, swing, point of contact, weight transfer, and follow through. If nothing seems to help, try changing your position on the baseline. Move two or three feet to your right or left, or even move back a few inches from the baseline. Sometimes a change of starting points can turn "out" serves into good serves. Practice serving. A few serves every fourth game in a weekly doubles match is not enough to develop and maintain a strong, consistent serve.

PREPARATION FOR GROUNDSTROKES

Making It Look Easy

One of the most common expressions heard from tennis spectators when they are watching advanced players is, "They really make it look easy." The reason good players make it look easy is that while most spectators are watching the ball being hit by one player, they do not see that the other player is working very hard to get into position for the next shot. By the time they look, the hitter has prepared so well that there is nothing left to do but swing at the ball. Getting ready to hit a shot is as important as actually hitting the ball when the time comes. The player who prepares well for each shot is always in a good tactical position on the court, is in a comfortable position to hit the ball, and is also positioned so that he can choose from a variety of alternatives on where and how to hit a return.

Hitting From a Stationary Position

Although most teachers and players learn to hit from a stationary position at first, very few shots are hit in such a way that a simple ready-pivot-step-swing sequence of movements is practical. Most of the time you have to run, shuffle, or move in some manner to be in a position to pivot, step, and swing. One of the few times when little lateral, forward, or backward movement is necessary is on the return of serve. Here are some suggestions on getting ready to hit that shot and others that come to where you are on the court.

First you must decide how you are going to hold the racket while you wait. The choices are a forehand grip, a backhand grip, an in-between grip, and the Continental grip. The technique for using various grips will be discussed later, but right now consider the factors involved in making the initial decision on which grip to use. If you hold the forehand grip while waiting, you are obviously going to be ready for a return on that side. If you think you have time to move so that the shot will be hit on the forehand side or if you anticipate most serves coming to that side, that may be the best grip for you. However, your grip must be changed considerably if the serve comes to your backhand, and that can be difficult for beginners and intermediates playing against an opponent with a fast serve. If you choose to hold a backhand grip while waiting for a serve, the same arguments apply. Some players have more trouble changing from forehand to backhand than from backhand to forehand. Either way the difference is going to be measured in fractions of seconds, but fractions of seconds are important in tennis. You may want to hold a grip that is halfway between the forehand and backhand grips. The advantage is that you are close to both grips, and the disadvantage is that you are going to have to adjust your grip on every return of serve. You could avoid this entire problem by holding a Continental grip for all groundstrokes, but this is used mostly by advanced players who have strong forearms or resilient rackets and strings.

Before deciding which method is best for you, answer these questions. (1) Which grip is most comfortable for you? (2) On which side do you expect most serves to come? (3) Is the forehand more difficult to change to than the backhand, or vice versa? If you answer yes to the last question, you may want to start out with the more difficult grip so you will have time prior to the serve to get the racket situated in your hand. If you still cannot decide what to do, take this advice: Wait for the serve with a backhand grip. Most beginning and intermediate players have more trouble with a shot to that side of the body, so they need all the time possible to get ready for it. Another reason is that most players are comfortable with a forehand grip and have little trouble changing into it when they have to in a hurry. Finally, many players will try to serve more frequently to your backhand, so be ready for them.

While waiting for the serve, hold the racket out in front of your body with the racket head pointing directly toward the server or slightly toward your backhand side. Use the nonracket hand to support the racket at the throat (the part between the head and the handle or grip). The racket should be far enough in front of you so that your weight is actually thrown forward a bit. This will force you to put your weight on your toes instead of your heels, a position that should help you react faster to any shot. Bend slightly at the knees and at the waist. Spread your feet a little wider than the width of your shoulders. Some players prefer to line their feet up evenly with the baseline, whereas others use a staggered stance. Be ready to leap out at the ball and attack it before it attacks you. The player in Figure 28 is demonstrating a position in which he is getting ready to return a serve.

Watch the ball being served from the time it leaves the server's hand until it reaches your racket strings. As soon as you see which side the ball is coming to, adjust your grip accordingly by moving the racket with the hand holding the racket at the throat; then move toward the ball by pivoting forward. If you are righthanded and the ball comes to your forehand, you should step forward and across the front of your body with the left foot (Figures 29 and 30). If the ball comes to your backhand side, the left foot is used as a pivot foot and the right foot moves forward (Figures 31 and 32). In either case, by the time you make the return, your feet should be aligned so that your toes form a line more or less parallel to the sideline. The foot closest to the net may be pointing at a 45-degree angle away from the baseline. This position makes it easier to move your weight forward as you hit. There are exceptions to the footwork just described, but worry about exceptions later. The player in Figures 30 and 32 has pivoted forward to hit a service return. Notice that the pivot foot has changed angles but that it is in the same place on the court as it was before the serve was delivered. Also remember that it is very rare for any shot to come at you so that a single pivot forward will put you into the correct hitting position.

Hitting on the Move

Most shots are hit on the run or after running to get into position. The latter is preferable. If you run first, set up second, and hit third, you are in a better position than most players. Ideally, you want to hit every groundstroke from approximately the same body position. The only way to achieve that goal is to get into position very quickly so you will have the luxury of hitting from a position in which you are comfortable.

There are a couple of ways to get to the ball. One way is to shuffle laterally. Instead of crossing your legs to move to one side, slide your feet alternately to the side where the ball is going. If you have to move to the right, first slide the right foot to the right and follow it by sliding the left foot. To do the same thing faster, use a skipping or hopping movement. The feet are still shuffling without crossing, but with a little bounce. If you really have to hurry to get to a ball in another part of the court, you simply have to turn and run. Use a crossover step as if you are going to pivot forward, and push off hard with the other foot.

Regardless of how you get to a ball, get there early and set up for the shot. Try to avoid arriving just in time to make contact with the ball. Pivot, shuffle, slide, or turn and run, but when you get there, plant the foot that is farther away from the net. Then shift your weight forward onto the other foot as you hit. If you have to get a short shot that bounces directly in front of you, move in to one side of the ball rather than going to it in a straight line.

Figure 28. In a ready position prior to returning a serve, the player's weight is forward, the racket pointing toward the server, and the knees flexed.

After each shot, start getting ready for the next one by (1) moving the racket back to the ready position in front of your body, and (2) positioning yourself in the best possible spot for the next return. For groundstrokes, that spot is usually at the center of the baseline, although it may change as the point progresses. As soon as you see where the next shot is coming, adjust your grip, get your racket back, and start moving toward the ball again. There is more to say about preparing to hit ground-strokes, but it will be said in separate discussions for the forehand and backhand.

FOREHAND

The Grip

Hold the racket with your left hand * so that one edge of the racket is pointing toward the floor or court (Figure 33). Now shake hands with

---

* Unless otherwise indicated, the instructions will be for righthanded players.

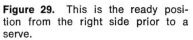

Figure 29. This is the ready position from the right side prior to a serve.

Figure 30. If the serve comes to the forehand side, the player pivots forward with the left foot. The forward pivot allows for a forward transfer of weight.

Figure 31 (left). Here is the ready position from another angle—the left side.

Figure 32 (right). When the serve comes to the backhand, the receiver pivots forward with the right foot to get his weight into the ball.

the racket just as if you were going to shake hands with another person. After you have grasped the racket, your hand should be in a position so that your fingers are curling around the grip near the base of it (Figure 34). Drop the racket to waist level, slightly adjusting your fingers on the grip to get a comfortable feel without changing the basic position of the racket in your hand. Your palm should be slightly behind the racket handle, your wrist should be in a position to give firm support from the rear of the racket handle, and the "V" formed by the thumb and index finger should be above but slightly toward the back part of the grip that faces upward. The back part of your hand should form a slight curve with the top of your forearm. That is the Eastern forehand grip (Figure 35).

While your dominant hand is holding the racket at the handle between shots, the opposite hand should be holding the racket at the throat. The racket must be held there to maintain an alert ready position, but it is also there to move the racket in your hand when you change from grip to grip during the course of a point. A player who does not feel comfortable with the opposite hand on the racket throat has not developed very far in tennis skills.

Figure 33 (left). Hold the racket with the non-racket hand. Point the edge of the racket toward the court.

Figure 34 (right). Now shake hands with the racket and your grip should look something like this.

Backswing

As soon as you know the ball is going to your forehand side, begin your backswing. The backswing is made by bringing the racket back either in a straight line parallel to the court or in a slight upward arc to a position where the racket is waist high and pointing to the fence behind the baseline (Figure 36). If the racket head can be seen behind your body by a person standing in front of you, it is probably too far back. Learn to run with your racket back behind your body. If you wait until you arrive at the ball to start your backswing, you will not have time to adjust to unexpected bounces, spin, or velocity. If the racket is already back there when you plant your feet, all you have to worry about is hitting.

Position of the Feet

Before you start the forward motion of your swing, try to plant the right foot (for a righthander), bend your knees slightly, and comfortably

Figure 35. The player has an Eastern forehand grip and the racket is back prior to the stroke.

separate the feet wider than shoulder width. Use the right foot to push off and transfer your weight forward as you begin to swing at the ball. As you hit, make sure that your weight has moved forward. Some players take a small step forward with the left foot just before they hit the ball. The most important part of any groundstroke is the forward weight transfer. If you do not put it into your stroke, you will be hitting only with power provided by your arm instead of with the entire weight of your body. The result is a lack of power and a very tired arm before the match or practice session has been completed. One way to determine if your weight is on the foot closer to the net is to be aware of the position of the shoulder closer to the net. If that shoulder is on a more or less even plane with the other shoulder or is in a downward posture, your weight is forward; if it is pointing up, your weight is still on the rear foot.

The Stroke Itself

As you swing at the ball, the racket should travel in a slightly upward arc. This upward and forward action of the racket allows you to hit with a slight amount of topspin, which is good for depth, a high bounce, and consistency. Keep the wrist in the position that forms a curve with the top of your forearm, and hold it firmly in place as you hit. Think of sweeping something off of a table or ironing board. Try to carry the ball on your racket strings. Hold the racket tightly enough so it will not turn in your hand on impact, but not so tightly that your knuckles turn white. Make

Figure 36. Take the racket back so that it is pointing toward the wall or fence behind you.

contact with the ball just before it reaches a point even with the mid-section of your body (Figure 37). Follow through outward toward the net and upward across your chest, in that order (Figure 38).

Every time you hit a forehand, the total action involved in the swing should be about the same. If the ball comes at you lower than the waist, bend the knees, keep your back straight, and use the same swinging motion. Do not stand straight up and golf at the ball. If you get caught in a position where the ball is going to bounce deeply in your back court and high to your forehand, retreat quickly, plant the back foot, and move your weight forward as you swing. If the ball falls short in your court, move up, plant, step, swing, and follow through.

As you improve your forehand, you can add to its effectiveness in a number of ways. Severe topspin can be a devastating offensive weapon and can be effected by taking a lower backswing than usual. Backspin can be put on the ball by starting the forward motion of the racket from a higher than normal position. Making contact with the ball at a variety of points within the forehand range can produce other effects. However, most of these techniques are effective for advanced players; before any additional forehand skills can be developed, first the fundamentals of the stroke have to be learned, practiced, and mastered.

Figure 37 (left). Lean into the ball and try to watch it leave your strings. Do not extend your arm quite as much on contact as this player is doing.

Figure 38 (right). Follow through up and across your chest.

Teaching Yourself How to Hit a Forehand

1. *Drop the ball with your left hand, simulate the forehand swing, and catch the ball with your right hand.* If you can do that easily, drop the ball, swing with the forehand motion, and hit the ball with the open hand. This exercise helps you develop the swinging motion and also requires you to watch the ball as you hit.

2. *Drop a ball to your forehand side and hit it over the net with a forehand stroke.* Turn your side to the net, extend your left arm and hand holding the ball, and drop the ball. Do not bounce it; just let it fall to the court. As it bounces up, lean forward and swing smoothly, aiming for a spot on the other side of the net.

3. *Holding the racket with a forehand grip, practice dribbling a tennis ball on the floor or court.* Beginners frequently have difficulty in getting used to the distance from the hand to the racket head. Dribbling the ball fifty to a hundred times a day not only helps you adjust to the

distance, it also makes the forehand grip seem like an automatic grip, and you may develop better racket control.

4. *With a forehand grip, turn your palm up and bounce the ball off the strings into the air as many times as you can without letting it touch the ground.* This drill improves ball control and strengthens the wrist. You should be able to hit at least one hundred consecutive air dribbles without a miss.

5. *Mark a court or open area at home with X's spaced several feet apart and to the right of a starting point. Practice getting into position by moving to a spot and executing a forehand swing.* Start from a central position, move alternately to each spot you have marked, plant your right foot, lean forward, and imagine you are swinging at and hitting a shot. After each shot, return to the starting point.

6. *Practice the forehand swing in front of a mirror.* Say to yourself, "Ready, pivot, swing," or "Ready, pivot, step, swing." Concentrate on watching each part of the stroke by itself, then watch the total movement. Attempt to develop a smooth, coordinated series of movements as you pretend to hit.

7. *Practice changing back and forth between the forehand and backhand grips.* You might also do this drill in front of a mirror. Repeat the grip changes so many times that you can change without looking at the racket. If you do not know how to hold the backhand grip, read the next part of this chapter before practicing this drill.

8. *Practice hitting forehands against a wall.* Stand very close to the wall at first and work on accuracy as well as form. Set goals for the number of consecutive hits without a miss. As you become more consistent, move progressively further away from the wall until you are finally at the distance from the baseline to the net (39 feet).

9. *Get a friend to throw balls to your forehand.* Take a basket of balls to the courts; have your friend stand about 20 feet away and use an underhanded toss that bounces easily about waist high. Begin your preparation from the ready position and pivot forward on each shot. As you get better, let the thrower toss balls away from where you are so you have to move, set up, then hit the shot. Return to a central position after every shot. This is another drill that can be used on any hard surface where there is enough open space in which to move and where there is a backstop to keep balls from getting away.

10. *Play a game with a friend using only the service courts.* Stand on or behind the service line and put the ball into play by dropping it and

softly hitting to your practice partner. Use short strokes. All shots must fall within the boundaries of the two service boxes. Keep score by counting the number of consecutive shots or by actually playing games using the conventional method of scoring.

11.   *From a position near the baseline, practice hitting forehands against a friend.* If both of you are righthanded, all shots will be hit crosscourt, from your forehand side to your opponent's. Set goals or count the number of consecutive shots played.

12.   *Hit down-the-line forehand shots only.* If your partner is good enough to keep the ball to your forehand side, hit fifty to one hundred shots with a forehand stroke so the ball travels parallel to the sideline. Concentrate on setting up early and hitting the ball deeply in your opponent's backcourt. If your friend is not good enough to hit all shots to your forehand, take turns throwing balls to the forehand.

13.   *Practice forehand strokes using only the alley on one side of the court.* All shots are directed toward the alley on the opposite side of the net. If you and your partner are both righthanded, he or she will have to either hit backhands on the return or move to the side of the court in order to practice forehand returns.

14.   *Practice forehand approach shots.* Ask your partner to throw or hit shots that bounce near the service line on your forehand side. Start from the center of the baseline, move in toward the ball, set up, and hit a forehand down the line on that side of the court.

15.   *Practice the forehand swing with a cover on the racket.* The added resistance will help improve your forearm and wrist strength.

16.   *Squeeze a tennis ball.* When you have some extra moments around the house or when your hands are free, hold an old tennis ball and squeeze it as hard as you can. Repeat 25 times and increase the number of consecutive squeezes by five each day. Your grip strength will improve significantly if you are conscientious about doing this exercise every day.

Recognizing and Solving Your Own Problems With the Forehand

1.   *Lack of power.* Are you getting your weight into the shot? If you are not, there are several possible reasons. Your feet may not be in proper position; turn your body so your feet are lined up more or less

parallel to the sideline. Your shoulder closest to the net may be pointing up; lean forward as you hit. You may be waiting too late to make contact with the ball; hit it before it gets even with you. You may not be following through; do not stop the forward motion of the racket when you hit, but carry the ball on the strings as far as possible by moving the racket outward toward the net and up across the front of your body.

2.   *Hitting out (beyond the baseline).* Always consider the possibility that you are swinging too hard. Anybody can hit hard. Only good players can hit crisp shots that stay inside the baseline. Also check the angle of the racket as you hit. If it is tilted too far up, the ball is going to bounce off the racket in the direction that your strings send it. A low backswing can also cause you to lift the ball up and out. Bring the racket back about waist high on the backswing.

Some players hit balls out because their opponents hit hard, fast returns. The harder your opponent hits, the less you should have to put into the return shot. Do not get into a slugging match with a hard hitter. Use his power by shortening your backswing and letting his power shots reflect off of your racket back to his court.

3.   *Hitting shots too far to your left if you are righthanded, or too much to the right if you are lefthanded.* There are only two causes for this problem. Your feet may not be lined up properly before you hit. As you pivot on one foot, the other foot should be brought around to a semi-closed stance (almost parallel to the sideline). If you are not doing that, you will pull the ball just as a righthanded baseball player pulls the ball down the left-field line when he steps into the bucket (steps to the side instead of in the direction where he wants to hit the ball). If that is not the problem, you are probably hitting the ball too early. Wait a bit longer before you make contact.

4.   *Hitting shots to your right (righthanders) or to your left (lefthanders).* You are waiting too late to hit the ball. Do not let it get past the midpoint of your body as you stand sideways to hit the forehand. You may be hitting late because you are not getting your racket back before the ball bounces on your side. Hurry up and then wait for it.

5.   *Shots always seem to be coming to your feet.* You are standing in the wrong place. Do not spend much time between the service line and the baseline. Some players want to move toward the net a step at a time. Caution is admirable, but if you move inside the baseline without going all the way to the service line or beyond, shots are naturally going to be bouncing close to your feet. Those shots are difficult for any player to

return. Either stay all the way back or move up to a position where you can volley.

6. *Your opponent seems to know where you are going to hit your forehand shots.* Think. Think far enough ahead during each point so you will know what he expects you to hit. If you know what he is expecting, do one of two things: either hit the shot so well that he cannot do anything about it, or hit to a spot on the court where he is not expecting you to hit. Vary your shots enough to keep your opponent honest, even if you occasionally hit a low-percentage shot (a more daring shot, not as likely to succeed as an easier shot).

7. *General inconsistency.* Poor preparation is always the first place to look for trouble. Poor preparation may be caused by poor concentration. Make sure you are hustling to get every shot instead of loafing in the direction of the next shot. A floppy wrist can also cause you to scatter the ball all over the place. Keep your wrist firmly in place as you swing forward. Do not let the racket turn in your hand as you hit. Watch the ball leave your racket strings. You may be looking up too soon. Practice. You cannot will shots into play; they have to be placed, and placement is the result of patient, regular practice.

BACKHAND

The backhand is one of the most difficult shots for many tennis players to master. There are tennis theorists who give detailed arguments why the backhand is a more natural stroke and should be easier to learn than the forehand. The arguments look good on paper, but on the courts it is another matter. People who have played other sports have had practice throwing, reaching, catching, pushing, hitting, and so on, but most of these movements are on the forehand side of the body. Very few sports involve the across-the-body action necessary to hit a backhand. Nevertheless, even though it is new and difficult for beginners and intermediates, it is a shot that can be learned, and furthermore, can become a consistent offensive weapon to add to your arsenal of strokes. Here's how.

The Grip

Put the racket on the floor or court. Reach down and pick it up so that your fingers curl around the base of the handle. Your little finger will be a fraction of an inch from the bottom of the grip. Cock your wrist up and hold the racket in front of your face so that you are looking through the strings (Figure 39). Without moving your wrist, turn the racket in your hand a quarter of a turn in either direction. Now you are looking at the edge of the racket head (Figure 40). Drop the racket to waist level and adjust your fingers to get a comfortable feel, moving your wrist slightly toward the back of the racket handle (Figure 41). Think of your thumb as having a top, bottom, outside, and inside. The inside part of your thumb should be in contact with the back, flat part of the racket grip (Figure 42). There are several ways in which the thumb might be aligned along that part of the grip, but it is essential that the inside part be in contact with the racket. During a point the thumb's position may change, but the part touching the grip should not. The grip you are holding is the Eastern backhand grip.

Many beginners want to hold the racket with the bottom part of the thumb in contact with the grip (Figure 43). This method of holding the backhand is popular because there is support behind the racket, but it is probably the single most important cause for some players never developing a strong backhand. The flat thumb grip is great for punching harmless little shots back across the net, but nothing more. It is terrible for low shots, it makes control difficult, and it limits the player in developing the backhand stroke beyond the beginner level.

Figure 39 (left).   Hold the racket up and look through the strings.

Figure 40 (right).   Turn the racket a quarter of a turn without moving your wrist so that you are looking at the edge of the racket.

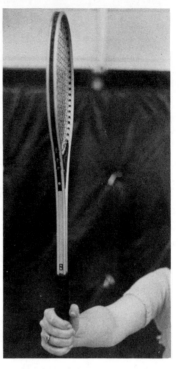

Figure 41 (above). Your wrist should be slightly behind the top of the racket handle.

Figure 42. This picture illustrates that the inside part of the thumb should be in contact with the grip. The thumb may be bent as it is here, or extended along the back of the grip.

Backswing

When you see the ball coming to your backhand, get the racket back as soon as you can. The racket should have been in the ready position prior to the shot, so your nonracket hand will be cradling the racket at the throat. Use that hand to turn the racket as you change to the backhand grip. Leave the left hand (if you are righthanded) on the racket throat during the entire backswing. Drawing the racket back with the left hand will keep everything in the proper plane for a smooth swing, and the hand will be there to give you added support as you begin the forward motion. As you bring the racket back, rotate your shoulders far enough back so that your opponent can see your back. The racket should come back in a

Figure 43. Never place the bottom part of the thumb in contact with the grip. This picture shows how **not** to hold the racket on the backhand.

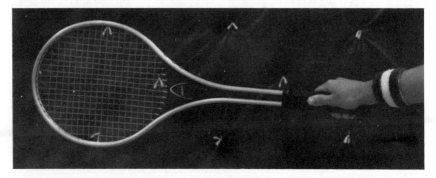

line parallel with the court or in a slight upward arc. It should be taken back at waist level, and it should be pointing at the fence behind you (Figure 44). As with the forehand, if a person standing in front of you can see the racket behind your body, you are probably taking too big a backswing. Learn to take a backswing as you move to hit the ball. Do not wait until the last second to prepare.

Position of the Feet

You have to turn before you hit so that your right shoulder is pointing in the direction you want to hit. On the backhand side, your left foot has to be set first, then your feet should again be separated comfortably, but wider than the width of your shoulders. Bend your knees slightly. The foot closer to the net may be pointing toward the sideline or it may be at a 45-degree angle to the baseline in the direction of the net. For added power take a small step forward with your right foot just before you hit. Put your weight into the shot as you swing. If your weight is on the back foot, shift forward to have the weight on the foot that is closer to the net when you hit. The right shoulder will be the key indicator of where your weight is. If the shoulder is up, your weight is on the rear foot; if the shoulder is down or in a level position, your weight is forward.

Figure 44. On the backswing, point the racket to the wall or fence behind the court.

The Stroke Itself

Swing in a trajectory parallel with the ground. Use the nonracket hand to push the racket from the backswung position forward. Lead the stroke with the racket head, not the wrist or elbow. If you use the grip described earlier and swing in the parallel trajectory, your racket should impart a slight backspin to your shot. Topspin on the backhand is effective, but it is a technique to be learned only after you have mastered the conventional backhand stroke. As you swing, rotate your shoulders in the same direction as you want to hit. The rotation will give you added power. Make contact with the ball at a point even with or in front of the foot that is closer to the net (Figure 45). Hitting the ball there will help you to use the pace provided by the other player and will lessen the stress put on your forearm as you hit. By hitting the ball before it gets even with you, you can hit with more power using less energy. Keep the elbow down and a few inches from your body as you swing. Extending it results in loss of power, and lifting it causes you to hit up on the ball. Follow through out, across, and up, in that order. Think of reaching out and touching the net with the back of your racket hand. When you have reached as far as you can in the direction of the net, bring the racket across the front of your

Figure 45. Lean into the ball and make contact with the ball before it gets even with you.

body and upward, finishing the stroke with the racket high on the right side (Figure 46).

The Two-Handed Backhand

The two-handed backhand has become a popular and effective stroke for many players. It has the advantages of giving you added power, a more controlled swing, and a better racket position to hit with topspin. Its disadvantage is that you may not be able to reach as far on wide shots as with the traditional backhand stroke. It could also hinder you from developing strength in your arm.

The grip with the right hand is the same as for the one-handed backhand. The left hand is also placed on the grip just above and in contact with the right hand. The left-hand grip should be similar to the Eastern forehand grip. Both hands should be placed on the grip as the backswing begins. The position of the feet should be about the same as for other backhand strokes, but some players use a more open stance with the two-

Figure 46. Follow through by reaching out, across, and up, in that order.

handed style, that is, the right foot is not brought around as far as it would be normally.

As you begin to swing forward, let the right hand do most of the work. The left hand is there for added wrist support and control. The rotation of the shoulders is easy because the hands and arms pull them through the shot. Make contact with the ball as it reaches the foot closer to the net. The follow through is also natural because the racket has to follow wherever the right hand pulls it. On very wide shots you may have to release the racket with the left hand as you hit.

If you decide to switch to a one-handed backhand from the two-handed style, the change ought not to be difficult. The basics of both strokes are the same. The player in Figures 47, 48, and 49 is shown after the backswing, making contact with the ball, and following through.

Teaching Yourself How to Hit a Backhand

Many of the methods used to teach yourself the forehand can also be used with the backhand. These methods will be listed without any

Figure 47 (left).   Point the racket directly to the wall or fence behind, holding the racket as this player is holding hers.

Figure 48 (right).   Make contact out in front.

additional comment, and other techniques for specifically developing the backhand will be given.

1. Practice up-in-the-air dribbles and dribbling against the court or floor with a backhand grip.

2. Mark an open area on the court with X's; move to each mark alternately, and swing through the backhand stroke.

3. Practice the backhand in front of a mirror.

4. Practice changing back and forth between the backhand and forehand grips.

5. Practice hitting backhands against a wall.

6. Get a friend to throw balls to your backhand.

7. Play the short game (service courts only) using backhands only.

8. Practice hitting only backhands against a friend.

9. Hit down-the-line backhand shots only.

10. Practice backhands using only one alley.

11. Practice backhand approach shots.

12. Practice the backhand swing with a cover on the racket.

Figure 49. Follow through out, across, and up. Holding the racket with two hands forces you to follow through in that direction.

13. Practice against a wall, hitting forehand and backhand strokes alternately. This "V" drill will help you develop both strokes and will also help you learn to change grips easily and quickly.

14. Attach a 3-pound weight to a cord; tie the cord to a stick; hold the stick, palms down with both hands; and roll the weight up. This exercise will strengthen your fingers, wrists, and forearms, making it easier for you to hit a backhand. The exercise is shown in Figure 50.

15. Get a friend to throw balls alternately to your backhand and forehand. The balls should be thrown far enough away from you so you have to run to get to each shot. As you hit one ball, the next one is thrown to the opposite side.

16. Practice an isometric backhand. At the point of probable contact with the ball on the backhand, push against an immovable object for three ten-second periods daily. Rest at least one minute between the exercise periods. In Figure 51 another person provides the resistance at the point of contact. This exercise can be used for all strokes.

Recognizing and Solving Your Own Problems With the Backhand

1. *Lack of power.* You may be hitting the ball too late. Concentrate on hitting the ball while it is on the rise and before it gets even with you.

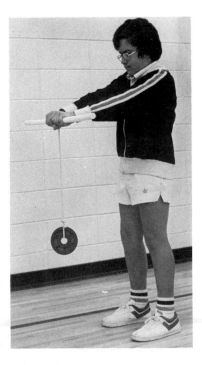

Figure 50. The wrist roll exercise will increase strength for any shot.

Figure 51. Push as hard as you can against an immovable object or another person. Use the muscles in your arm instead of just leaning into the stroke with your body.

Hitting too late puts a strain on the forearm and wrist, and usually causes a weak return. In order to hit the ball in front of you, set up early. Move into position with the racket back, plant the left foot, and use the opposite hand to push the racket forward. Your weight should be on the foot that is closer to the net when you hit. Be sure to follow through with your swing. Punching at a backhand will result in a weak shot just as punching at a forehand without following through will.

2. *Hitting the ball up and out beyond the baseline.* First, check your grip to make sure the racket angle will allow you to put a little backspin on the ball. Then analyze your swing to see if the motion of your racket is parallel to the court. Bend your knees and do not hit the ball too hard. Finally, keep the shoulder that is closer to the net level. If it is lifted, you will probably lift the ball.

3. *Hitting too far to the right.* The same things that cause the ball to go to the left on the forehand will cause you to hit to the right on the

backhand. Either you are not bringing the right foot far enough around as you turn prior to hitting, or you are swinging and making contact with the ball too early.

4.   *Hitting out to the left side of the court.* Swinging late and making contact late will both cause this problem. Avoid too lengthy a backswing. Another possible cause is stepping too far across with your right foot as you prepare to hit. A crossover step that is too big can throw you off balance.

5.   *General inconsistency.* Keep the wrist firmly in place. Do not let it flop or droop when you hit a backhand. The racket head should always be held higher than the wrist. Remember to cock the wrist up and hold the racket tightly. Most of the backhand movement takes place at the shoulder joint. Too much flexion at other joints can cause you to spray shots in all directions.

VOLLEY

The volley is an easy shot to learn in practice, but it can be a difficult one to hit in a match. You can teach yourself this stroke more easily than some other strokes because there is one grip for volleys, regardless of where they are hit, and because the shot does not require a full swing. This can be an advantage in that the less motion in a swing, the fewer chances there are for an error. However, the stroke can give you problems in a match because you have less time to react than you would on shots returned from the baseline.

The volley is one of the most challenging and exciting strokes in tennis. If you are in a position to volley, you are probably playing offensive tennis, which is more fun than defensive tennis for many players. If you can volley, you can take charge of a point, put pressure on your opponent, and cut the court space in half just as a boxer cuts the ring in half for his opponent.

The Grip

Put the racket on the floor or court. Reach down and pick the racket up, holding it at the base of the grip so that your fingers curl around the handle. As with other grips, your little finger should be about a half inch from the bottom of the handle. Cock your wrist and hold the racket in front of you so that you are looking through the strings (Figure 52). Turn the racket 90 degrees in either direction without moving your wrist or fingers. Now you are looking at the edge of the racket head (Figure 53).

Move your fingers to get a firm, comfortable grip without changing the angle at which you are holding the racket. Bend your elbow slightly and drop your arm so the racket is still in front or you but at chest level. The grip you are holding (Figure 54) is called the Continental grip and it is used for all volleys—right side, left side, high, and low. Some teachers allow their students to change grips at the net until the Continental grip is comfortable. This grip is very similar to the Eastern backhand grip. With the Continental grip, when you volley on your backhand side, you should feel relatively comfortable with the way you are holding the racket. Your thumb is behind the racket handle to give you plenty of support. Shots that come to your forehand will give you more problems and make you feel uncomfortable at first. You will get used to the feeling, so don't give up on the grip. The reason you cannot change grips is because you simply do not have time to change back and forth between grips when you are at the net. Since you have to hold the racket with only one grip, experience has proven that you can hit a forehand volley more effectively with a near-backhand grip (Continental) than you can hit a backhand volley with an Eastern forehand grip. If that all sounds confusing, forget the reasoning and just hold the racket as shown in the illustrations. After it works for you, the reasons will not matter.

Position of the Feet

First, you have to decide where to stand for volleys. With the serve and groundstrokes, you stand where you have to stand, that is, wherever you want to serve from or wherever balls are hit on your side of the court. With the volley, you can have more freedom to position yourself, and your position will depend on what is happening during each point. This freedom—or problem, depending on how you look at it—will be discussed more thoroughly in the section on strategy. If you are learning to hit the volley, it is probably best to practice standing 6 to 8 feet from the net. At that distance you will have to volley the ball with some force, but you will still be close enough to the net to allow for a few errors in pace or direction while still keeping the ball in play.

Your feet should be spread wider than the width of your shoulders and firmly placed so you can push off at an angle in the direction of the net. Your weight should be thrown forward so your heels are barely in contact with the court, if in contact at all. Bend your knees enough to get the feeling of hitting out of a crouch. You should also bend slightly forward at the waist. As the ball approaches, you want to be in a position to spring out for the shot.

If the ball comes to your right side, use the right foot to pivot, and step across and toward the net at a 45-degree angle with your left foot

Figure 52 (left). Look through the strings, holding the racket like this.

Figure 53 (right). Turn the racket 90 degrees in your hand so that you look at the racket's edge.

Figure 54. Drop your arms, use the Continental grip, and assume a ready position at the net.

(Figure 55). Concentrate on moving forward instead of moving laterally along the net or pivoting in reverse. If the ball comes to your left side, pivot on the left foot and step across and into the ball with the right foot (Figure 56).

If the ball comes directly at you, the footwork is different. You can move in either direction, but you have to slide to one side of the path of the ball. You do that by pushing off with one foot and sliding the opposite foot away from it at about a 45-degree angle to the net. For example, if you are righthanded and the ball comes straight at you, you might push off with the right foot, taking a step at an angle toward the net with your left foot. That would put you in a position to hit the ball with a forehand volley (Figure 57).

Backswing

The backswing for the volley on either side is a short, restricted motion. The movement begins from a ready position in which you are carrying the racket up and in front of you. The racket is cradled at the throat with one hand and is pointing toward your opponent or slightly to your backhand side. As you see the ball coming, the racket is brought back to a point not much further back than an imaginary line even with you and parallel to the net. If a person were to stand on the side opposite of your racket hand, he should not be able to see the racket brought back behind your body. Rotate your shoulders in the direction of the backswing. The idea is to take a short, quick, controlled backswing because you do not have time to take a full swing at the ball.

The Stroke Itself

Throughout the volleying motion, keep your wrist cocked so that the racket forms a near 90-degree angle with your forearm. Lead the stroke with the racket head. Swing forward from the shoulder and elbow, but keep your wrist in a fixed position. Make contact with the ball well in front of your body. Try to hit the ball while it is on the rise. On a volley it is essential to attack the ball rather than letting it get even with or behind you. If you have stepped forward, your weight should be on the foot closer to the net. The shoulder closer to the net should be down. Direct your volleys deep into the backcourt of your opponent or at an angle to pull him off the court. Remember: racket out in front while waiting; weight forward; short backswing; and hit the ball before it gets even with you. Follow through fully in the direction in which you want to hit the ball.

Figure 55. Pivot forward with your left foot for volleys on the forehand side.

Figure 56. On the backhand volleys, try to step forward and into the ball with the right foot.

Figure 57. On balls that come straight at you, step forward at a slight angle with one foot and bring your racket up to block the ball.

To be extra alert, many players crouch low and bounce on the balls of their feet when they expect a shot to be hit at them. If the shot comes to you low, do not stand straight up and put your racket down to hit the volley. Bend your knees even more and get down to eye level with the ball. The angle of the racket will be the same as on any other volley because you are bending your knees instead of bending at the waist or dropping the racket head. One object of the volley is to avoid volleying up on the ball. If you volley up, your opponent will be in a position to hit down on the return.

The player in Figures 58 and 59 is shown in the ready position, making contact with the ball, and following through after the volley.

Teaching Yourself How to Hit the Volley

There are very few drills or exercises for the volley which can be done alone. Most of the time you will need a friend to throw or hit balls to you.

1. *Practice in front of a mirror.* As with any other shot, you may be able to perfect your volley motion by watching yourself swing. Look for one component at a time, then watch yourself move through the whole stroke several times on each side of your body.

2. *Practice catching a tossed ball with the racket.* Have a friend toss to you, and instead of hitting at the ball, just reach out with the racket and "catch" it. The ball will often rebound off your racket with enough force to cross the net. If not, you will at least get used to the distance between the hand and the racket head. The drill will also give you a good start toward punching at the ball rather than swinging at it.

3. *Return tossed balls with volleys.* Have your partner throw softly to the forehand side only, later switching to the backhand. Volley the shots back in order to avoid having to chase balls. After you have become comfortable in hitting at the net, ask the thrower to mix up the tosses between the forehand and backhand sides.

4. *Volley from a position near the fence or wall surrounding the court.* To force yourself to take short backswings on volleys, stand near the fence or wall and have someone throw to you. If you take too big a backswing, your racket will bump the fence. Shorten the swing if that happens.

5. *Volley from a position in a doorway or gate opening.* This exercise forces you to step forward as you hit the volley. If you do not step into the ball, your racket will hit the sides of the door or gate.

Figure 58 (left). Ready position at the net.

Figure 59 (right). Make contact with the ball well in front of the body on volleys.

6. *Volley toward a target on the court.* Place tennis ball cans or racket covers in spots on the court and direct your volleys to those spots. Work on hitting crosscourt volleys.

7. *Take a volleying position, have your partner hit shots at you, but call the balls "in" or "out" without hitting and before the balls bounce.* Many beginners have trouble judging whether or not shots are going to be in the court or out. This drill helps you to improve your judgment of shots. You will need a basket of balls to do this drill effectively.

8. *Count the number of consecutive volleys you and a friend can hit.* You will have to reach an intermediate or advanced level before you can control the ball well enough to do this drill.

9. *Volley against two friends who alternately hit shots to you at the net.* The two against one drill enables you to hit many volleys in a short period of time. Rotate so that each player gets a turn at the net.

10. *Stand in the service court near the net and move as fast as you can back and forth from the singles sideline to the midcourt line ten*

times. Swing through the volley motion every time you reach a line. Try to increase the number of repetitions each time you do the drill. This is a good conditioning exercise.

11. *Hit volleys against a wall or rebound net.* This is not a drill for beginners. Intermediates may be able to keep the ball in play long enough to make the drill worthwhile.

12. *Stand in one service court near the net, and defend that area with volleys.* Your practice partner will drop and hit or return your volleys with attempted passing shots. Your goal is to return any shot that would fall within the boundaries formed by the center service line and the singles sideline.

Recognizing and Solving Your Own Problems With the Volley

1. *Lack of power.* You may not be holding the racket tightly enough. At the net, balls are coming at you faster than in the backcourt. If you are not gripping tightly, the force of the shot may turn the racket in your hand, resulting in a weak volley.

The same problems that cause a lack of power in groundstrokes can cause you to hit powerless volleys. These problems include not stepping forward to hit, not meeting the ball on the rise and in front of you, and not following through with the swing. Also consider the possibility that you are standing too far from the net. Some of the pace you are putting on the ball may be taken off by the distance you are trying to hit.

2. *Hitting volleys out (beyond the baseline).* This problem will not be as common with the volley as with other strokes. If you are hitting balls out, you may be swinging at the volley instead of punching at it with a short backswing. An incorrect grip can also cause you to hit up and out, so check to see if you are holding the racket with a Continental grip on both the forehand and backhand sides.

3. *Hitting wide to either side of the court.* As with the ground-strokes, the cause could be either hitting the ball too soon (which is doubtful on volleys), hitting too late (which is more likely to happen), not turning your shoulders as you prepare, or using too much wrist in your stroke.

4. *General inconsistency.* Keep the racket head up. Letting it drop below the level of the wrist will cause you to net many balls. Watch the ball. That is easy to say, but hard to do when the time comes. Try to focus on the ball all the way in to your racket strings. Do not try to put every

volley away. You will make fewer errors if you attempt a good placement on the first volley and get the ball past your opponent on the second one. Many players hit volleys out because they should not be hitting volleys at all. Read the section on strategy to learn when you should advance to the net.

OVERHEAD SMASH

If you have been waiting to read about the one shot in tennis in which you can really let out and hit as hard as you want to every time, the overhead smash is not it. At least not most of the time. One of the problems beginners and intermediates have with the overhead smash is knowing when to attempt a put-away and when to go for placement instead of power. The guideline to follow is determined by where you are on the court when your opponent hits a lob. If the ball is going to be smashed from a position in the forecourt (from the service line forward), the put-away can be tried, assuming that you are capable of putting a ball away. But if you are preparing to return a lob and you are standing close to or behind your own baseline, a put-away smash should seldom be attempted. The reasons are easy to understand, but some players just cannot resist the temptation to blast every lob hit to them, even when the odds are slim that the shot will be successful. From the baseline, it is very difficult to hit an outright winner. The distance is too far, the angle is poor because of the increased distance between you and the other player, and your opponent has too much time to react to your shot. So instead of hitting an all-out smash, you should hit the overhead firmly and deeply to an open spot or to your opponent's weakness. If your shot is hit well, the next shot might be a winner.

Before considering the mechanics of hitting the smash, there is one other decision that has to be made before the shot is hit. That problem is whether to hit the overhead before or after the ball has bounced. Unless you are an advanced player, try this method for making your decision. If you can allow the ball to bounce without giving up more than two or three steps toward your baseline before you hit, the ball should be played off the bounce. The chance for a put-away is smaller, but the shot will be safer because there is more time to prepare and because the bounce will minimize factors such as wind, velocity, and spin. If you see that by letting the ball bounce you will have to retreat more than two or three steps toward your baseline, hit the ball before it bounces. There is a greater risk of missing the shot because of the variables mentioned earlier, but it is better to take that risk than to have to fall back too deeply to make an effective return. If there is a doubt about what to do, the shot should be played after the ball has bounced. Indecision can ruin any stroke in tennis.

The Grip

The grip used for the overhead smash should be similar to the backhand grip or to a Continental grip. Hitting a smash with that kind of grip will feel very uncomfortable at first, but you have to do it that way to develop an effective smash. Since the grip is like the one used to hit a backhand, and since the overhead is hit on the forehand side of the body, some adjustments have to be made as the ball is hit. The primary adjustment is made by rotating the wrist outward as you strike the ball. An outward rotation means that, looking at the back of your hand, the thumb goes away from you, down, and across. This pronation type of movement allows you to hit the ball flat (with little spin) and with more force than you put on groundstrokes. The inward and downward snap of the thumb and forearm puts added zip on the ball. If you do not rotate the wrist in this manner, the shot you hit will have too much spin and probably go off too far to the righthander's left side. The ball will also be hit with less velocity, which is particularly bad for the smash.

Position of the Feet

Failure to move the feet during preparation for the overhead shot is one of the most common errors made by players at all levels. Too many players see a lob coming, dig in to a fixed position with both feet, then try to hit. The problem is that since lobs are in the air longer than other shots, all of the variables such as velocity, spin, and trajectory may change during the flight of the ball. If you get set too soon, you might misread some of the variables and not adjust accordingly. Take several short, half and quarter steps while preparing for the overhead. A lot of foot movement will help you to be in the perfect position to hit when the time comes.

If you have to move back to hit an overhead, retreat in a sideways body position. Turn your left shoulder to the net (if you are a righthander), move back rapidly, and plant your right foot. As you hit, you will still be pushing off with the right foot and transferring your weight forward to the left one. If your feet are parallel to the net when you hit, you cannot shift your weight forward. So when you swing, the right foot will be away from the net and the left one will be closer to the net.

Backswing

Bring the racket directly up in front of your body to a position behind your head as you prepare to hit. If you were to take a full swing, you would drop the racket down and bring it up behind the back in a pendulum-like motion. By eliminating the full swing, you can reduce the margin of error. If your position on the court is good enough, you should still have enough power to put the shot away or to hit a strong placement. The full backswing can give you a more powerful motion, but it will be less efficient and less accurate than the restricted backswing. As you bring the racket back behind your head, point to the ball with the opposite hand. Pointing to the ball can improve your concentration, and it will make you more aware of your position in relation to the ball. If you are pointing to the ball, you should also be able to make contact at the spot where you are pointing. You want to do that because the point of contact will be in front of you, forcing you to move your weight into the ball.

The Stroke Itself

The smashing motion is similar to a forceful punch serve. You already have the racket behind your head, so bring it forward as if throwing your racket across the net. As you swing, make sure that your weight is forward and moving into the ball. As you hit, your weight should be on the foot closer to the net. Hit the ball at a point in front of you (Figure 60). As you hit, rotate the wrist outward and snap down with the thumb as much as possible. If you are close to the net, hit the ball with as little spin as you can to get maximum velocity. If you are at midcourt, use some spin to make the ball curve down and into the court. If you are in your backcourt or behind the baseline, put even more spin on the shot. The distance between you and the net is too far for a flat shot to be effective. Follow through down and across your body, but do not worry about taking a full follow through as you would on the serve. Bring the racket through the stroke naturally, then return it to the ready position for the next shot.

Teaching Yourself How to
Hit an Overhead Smash

Very few tennis players take the time to perfect this shot in practice. Most people hit a few during the warmup before the match and then take their chances on hitting good smashes during the match. Only outstanding athletes are gifted enough to get by with such limited practice. Most of us should hit 25 to 50 overheads every time we go out to play. If you do not have the time to put in that kind of practice, do not expect to develop a strong overhead.

If you have a basket of balls and can get together with a friend, take turns lobbing to each other. Stand very close to the net at first and

Figure 60. Make contact in front of your body on the overhead smash.

have your practice partner feed you very soft, easy lobs. Take your time, get set, and get the feel of hitting deep, crisp smashes at close range. When you feel comfortable and confident at the net, gradually move back to positions deeper in the court. At midcourt, you will get practice judging whether to play the ball in the air or after the bounce, as well as hitting smashes at longer distances. If your partner is good enough, use a lob and smash drill, in which you hit smashes and the other player lobs as long as you can keep the ball in play. Change roles after each player has hit ten to fifteen smashes. Also practice smashing to different spots on the court. Place racket covers or cans on the court and try to hit them. If you can do that, try smashing to a spot left open by your opponent. This drill will force you to hit with direction while being aware of the court position of your opponent.

Recognizing and Solving Your Own Problems With the Overhead Smash

1. *Lack of power.* You have to have a degree of strength to hit this shot, so don't expect too much from too little. Good timing can compensate for lack of strength, however. Be sure you are in a position on the court to hit a powerful smash. Very few players can hit strong overheads from deep in their backcourt. You may be trying to hit too much of a shot. Is your weight forward as you hit? A common error with this stroke is leaning backward as the ball is hit. If you are doing that, you cannot be hitting with much force. Point at the ball with one hand and make contact where you point. Do not let the ball get directly over or behind your head. Check the position of your feet. Remember that the feet have to be in a staggered position in order for you to shift your weight into the ball.

2. *Hitting out (beyond the baseline).* You are probably not swinging down on the ball or you are not rotating the wrist forward and down as you hit. A stiff, inflexible wrist on this shot will cause the racket to face out or up, and the ball will go in the direction the racket face points. Don't hit too hard. Be content to set your opponent up with the first smash and to put your opponent and the ball away on the next shot.

3. *Hitting into the net.* This is another frequent problem, even when the hitter is hitting with power. The usual cause is that the wrist is breaking too soon. Practicing at midcourt and backcourt should correct this fault. Part of the problem is just getting used to the distance with which you have to work.

4. *Hitting wide to the left (righthanders).* Check your grip to see if you are still holding something close to a backhand grip. If you are, concentrate on rotating the wrist out as you hit. If you do not do this, you will hit with too much spin and the spin will carry the ball across and out. Hitting wide to the right has no obvious cause other than taking your eyes off the ball before you hit.

5. *General inconsistency.* Get set early. Move your feet in short, choppy steps and get your racket back behind your head while you move into position. Waiting until the last second to prepare will cause inconsistency with any stroke, especially the overhead smash. Shorten your swing. Big windups increase the possibility of errors at all points in the swinging motion. Reduce the motion and reduce the errors. Watch the ball until it hits your racket strings. Practice. At the very least, ask your opponent to give you five to ten lobs during a pre-match warmup period.

THE LOB

Like the overhead smash, the lob is one of the game's most valuable shots, but one which players seldom take the time to practice and refine. The shot is effective as an offensive weapon, as a defensive technique, and as a way to keep your opponent off balance. The lob is not something you use only when you are in trouble. It should be used any time it will help you win a point, and that is usually much more often than most players realize.

The Grip and Footwork

As an offensive shot, the lob can be used when your opponent has moved into a volleying position near the net, when you are returning the ball in singles against an opponent who follows his serve to the net, and occasionally when you are returning a serve down the line and over the net player's head in doubles. In all of these instances, the grip you use should be the same one that you use for either the forehand or backhand. The position of the feet is also the same. The lob is most effective when your opponent is not expecting it, so it should start out looking like any other groundstroke. If you change your grip or the position of your feet from the way you normally prepare for a shot, your opponent will be able to anticipate what you are going to do.

The Backswing and the Stroke Itself

The way you swing at the ball on a lob will be different from that of other shots, especially on offensive lobs. Advanced players frequently hit a topspin lob, but the shot is too sophisticated for beginners and intermediates. If you are going to hit an offensive lob with backspin, your backswing should be a little shorter than on other groundstrokes. The shorter swing is used not to make the shot more effective, but simply because you probably will not have time to take a full backswing against the kind of forcing shot your opponent will hit as he or she comes to the net. Open the face of your racket as you hit so that the shot has backspin, but wait as long as you can to tilt the face upward. The point of contact may be further back than on other shots because you are returning a forcing shot and because if you can wait another fraction of a second, your opponent will be committed even further toward the net. With the open racket face, chip the ball upward and aim it high enough to clear your opponent's outstretched racket. The ball should be hit high enough so that it cannot be played before the bounce and low enough so that it cannot be reached after the bounce. Direct the ball to the backhand side of the net player whenever possible. The follow through should also be a bit shorter than on other baseline strokes.

The more commonly used lob is a defensive shot used to keep a point going rather than to win it. When you hit this shot you are probably either running, out of position, off balance, or generally in trouble. Technique is not quite as important when you are scrambling to stay alive in a rally, but technique should not be overlooked. First, run with the racket back if you can. Now, more than on any other shot, you do not have time for stroke preparation at the last second. Second, use a sweeping, lifting motion with your arm and racket as you hit and put the ball high into the air. Try to carry the ball on the strings and "baby it" back across the net with backspin. You want to get the ball well into the air so you will have time to recover and get back into position to return the next shot. If you can, lob to your opponent's backhand. Follow through fully —up, out, and across your body, in that order. The full follow through will help you get the feel of gently lifting the ball up into the air and deep into the backcourt. Hold on to the racket tightly throughout the stroke. You need a firm grip to return a hard hit shot and to acquire the touch necessary for a delicate shot.

Teaching Yourself to Hit the Lob

You need someone to throw or hit balls to you to develop this stroke. Dropping a ball and hitting lobs does not simulate game conditions. At first, stay on or just behind the baseline and return the ball with lobs to get the feel of the shot and to get used to the height and distance needed to make the shot effective. Then practice the offensive lob by attempting to barely clear the player at the net. If you hit short, the net player can practice the overhead smash. There you have a three-shot drill: (1) net player hits a deep, forcing shot; (2) you return with a lob; (3) if the lob falls short, the drill ends with a smash; if your lob clears the net player, the drill begins again. After you have become accustomed to the feel and trajectory of the shot, work on placing the ball either to different spots on the court or to your opponent's backhand. The last stage is to learn to hit the lob while running. Have your practice partner toss balls alternately to each corner of your backcourt. Retrieve the first ball with a forehand, hitting high and deep, then head for the opposite corner of the backcourt to hit the next ball with a backhand lob. This drill will improve your physical condition as well as your lob.

Finally, use game and match situations to practice lobbing. If you are playing an informal match, use the lob more often than you would normally, even if a groundstroke might be more appropriate. Losing a few points in friendly matches for the sake of practice might result in a point-winning stroke in a tournament.

Recognizing and Solving Your Own Problems With the Lob

1. *Hitting out (beyond the baseline).* Take the wind into consideration. Lobbing with the wind at your back is safe in terms of not setting up your opponent for a smash, but the ball can easily be carried out by the wind. Sometimes the wind currents are stronger above the level of the fence surrounding the court than at ground level. What may seem like a well-placed shot may take off when it gets higher into the air.

You could also be hitting too hard or too soon. The lob is one of the most delicate shots in the game. If you get too much weight, arm, or wrist into the motion, you will lose control. Wait until the ball is even with you to make contact. Be sure to put backspin on the ball; that will make it slow down in the air instead of sailing beyond the baseline. Give yourself room to lob. If you are on defense, play behind the baseline two or three steps. That will give you more time to react and more space to work within on your return.

2. *Hitting too short.* A short lob is an embarrassing shot because your opponent will probably put it away with an eye-catching smash. Be careful about lobbing into the wind. Seemingly good lobs can be slowed enough by the wind to fall right into your opponent's overhead smash. Hold on to your racket tightly. Do not let the force of the ball jar the racket in your hand and cause a weak return. Follow through on defensive lobs. Jabbing at the ball may cause you to pop it up short. Do not forget fundamentals of footwork and preparation. A position squarely facing the net prevents you from getting anything but your arm into the ball, and you arm may not be enough.

3. *General inconsistency.* Watch the ball. Do not waste your energy in running down the shot only to hit it wide because you did not watch the ball all the way into your racket strings. Check the angle of the racket face as you hit. The ball goes where your racket face tells it to go, so be aware of the angle at which the ball reflects off the strings. Direct your lobs to a spot or an area of the court instead of being content to just get the ball back. That will help you concentrate on the shot. Use the stroke more frequently than you do now. You cannot expect consistency with any shot unless you hit it regularly.

THE DROP SHOT

Drop shots should be used from a position inside the service line. Drop shots hit from further back in the court look good when they are successful, but the odds are against those shots being successful very often. Use the shot when your opponent is too far out of position behind the baseline, when he is off to either side of the court, or when he is on his heels expecting a forcing shot. The shot is most effective against opponents who are either slow or out of shape. The slow ones may not be able to get to the ball, and the players in poor condition will tire if you make them run enough. Hit the drop shot often enough to make your opponents think about the possibility that you might use the shot regularly. If they have to worry about possible drop shots, your other shots from similar positions on the court may become even more effective.

Preparation and Execution

Disguise the drop shot. It should look like you are going to hit any other shot you might use from the forecourt. This means that there should be no exaggerated backswing, no delay in the stroke, no change in footwork, and no difference in facial expression. Hold the racket firmly, and delicately slide the racket face under the ball as you make contact. Shots played after the bounce require a full, smooth follow through. Drop volleys are usually more effective if the follow through is abbreviated. Be especially careful to bend your knees and hit out of a crouched position.

Hit the drop shot so that the ball is falling in a downward direction as it clears the net. Barely clearing the net is effective, but not absolutely necessary. The thing to avoid is hitting the ball so that it travels too far in a horizontal plane after the bounce. Putting backspin on the ball should make it bite into the court and not travel far toward the baseline. Expect your opponent to reach the ball and return it. If he does not get to it, you still win the point; if he does, you should be right in front of him and near the net, ready to volley the return for a winner. Hitting drop shots on consecutive points may be a good idea if your opponent really has to work hard to get to the ball on the first attempted return.

Teaching Yourself How to
Hit the Drop Shot

Have your practice partner drop and hit baseline drives to you at the net. Get the feel of the shot at first and work on direction and placement second. Playing short games and drop shot games can also help you to improve this stroke. Short games are played with two, three, or four people who use the service line as the back boundary. If there are three people, play two against one. Anything hit deeper than midcourt is out. Drop shot games can be played with lines marked 6 feet from and parallel to the net on each side. All shots must be drop shots and all must fall on or within the marked lines. Keep score as you would in a regular match.

Recognizing and Solving Your Own Problems With the Drop Shot

1. *Hitting too deeply.* You may be putting too much swing or follow through into a drop volley. Punch at the ball and bring the racket under it. Lack of backspin will cause the ball to bounce deeper than it should. Make the shot travel in a trajectory whose path looks like a hairpin, not like a footbridge. Do not use the drop shot when the wind is with you: there is too great a risk of the ball's being carried in the direction of your opponent. Do not stand too close to the net. Give yourself room to hit the shot.

2. *General inconsistency.* Hold the racket firmly to feel the shot. You want to "baby" the ball across the net, but you have to hold the racket tightly to hit a precision shot like this one. Get down with the ball before you hit and as you hit. Standing straight up and dropping the racket head down to hit this or any other shot will cause problems.

3. *Telegraphing the shot.* Ask your practice partner if he or she knows when you are going to hit the drop. If so, try to identify the mannerisms you exhibit before the shot and work on eliminating them.

In this section, seven basic strokes have been discussed: the serve, forehand, backhand, volley, overhead smash, lob, and drop shot. There are several other specialized shots which will not be discussed. The American twist serve, the lob volley, and the half volley are examples. These and other strokes are used primarily by advanced players who have mastered the basic shots. The beginning and intermediate players are probably better off not being mentally overloaded with detailed explanations about shots they are not ready to put into use.

3

Developing Strategy

INTRODUCTION

Tennis strategy is a general plan or method that a player uses to try to defeat an opponent. The best strategy for beginners is to hit shots as they are supposed to be hit and to keep the ball in play. Until you can direct the ball to areas of the court and use a variety of strokes effectively, there is no need to become overly concerned about strategy. There is some strategy involved in court position for the beginner, and that will be discussed in this section. Once you begin to have a reasonable degree of control over your strokes, you can think beyond merely hitting the ball. If you are already at that level, you have probably advanced out of the beginner level and can call yourself an intermediate tennis player.

Most of the information in this chapter is for the intermediate player. Some material will even apply to advanced players because many principles of strategy should be followed by anyone who plays the game beyond the basic level. If you are a beginner, read this section but consider the suggestions as goals to be reached later in your tennis life. Later could be next month or next year. There is no clear dividing line between the advanced beginner and the intermediate player. You will gradually grow into more sophisticated levels of play before finally leveling out. The growth may be segmented in the sense that one stroke may become very strong while other parts of your game remain relatively weak. Knowing how and when to use each part of your game effectively will be good information to have when the time comes for you to develop your game further.

SINGLES

Playing Low-Risk Tennis [1]

Any discussion of developing singles strategy or a game plan has to include comments on low-risk, percentage tennis. Percentage tennis might also be called smart tennis, safe tennis, and if properly executed, winning tennis. The concept means that there are certain shots that should be hit in certain situations during the course of a point or game. If these are hit well, the hitter will win that point or be in a position to win the point a high percentage of the time. It does not necessarily mean that these percentage shots should be tried 100 percent of the time. If you fall into a pattern that your opponent can predict, he will have an easier time anticipating the next shot and winning the point himself. Occasionally, hitting the nonpercentage shot will win the point; if not, it will at least keep the opponent honest. It will also add a little more fun to the game. However, over a long period of time, hitting the shot that the situation calls for yields positive results. The tennis player who hits the smart percentage shot is saying, "I'm going to put this shot right where the book says it should go, and there is not much you will be able to do about it."

Playing low-risk tennis requires a disciplined player. First, you must spend enough time in practice to develop the most effective shots. For example, the low, down-the-line approach shot does not come automatically. The shot must be practiced repeatedly in order for you to use it effectively in a match. All the knowledge in the world about percentage tennis will not help you if you cannot hit the required shot when you need it. If you are not disciplined enough to spend the hours of practice necessary to perfect percentage shots, you will probably lose. Second, playing low-risk tennis may take some of the fun out of the game for some players. Part of the appeal of tennis is the challenge of making a spectacular shot. Most percentage shots are not spectacular; they are shots designed to set up an opponent for a slow kill. Again, it takes discipline for a player to pass up a chance to hit a great shot in favor of hitting an everyday shot. Some people can never make that adjustment: they are destined to play a few spectacular points, games, or even matches, but to lose more than they win over the long run. The challenge for the percentage player is in winning, not the shot making.

[1] Jim Brown, *Tennis: Teaching, Coaching, and Directing Programs* (Englewood Cliffs, N.J.: Prentice-Hall, Inc., 1976), 26.

The first rule of percentage tennis is to keep the ball in play. If you can do that as a beginner, you are already playing at a higher intellectual level than some players who have better strokes than you do. In spite of the advice given by tennis teachers for decades, about 75 percent of all points are lost by errors rather than won by good shots. The idea of the game is to hit the ball over the net and in bounds one more time than your opponent on each point. You do not have to hit the ball harder, lower, with more spin, or at a sharper angle; just hit it over and in a little more often than your opponent does.

Keeping the ball in play requires that you cut down on the number of unnecessary errors. Is there such a thing as a necessary error? There may be, at least in the sense that some errors are forced by an opponent who puts you in a position of trying a difficult shot or hitting an easy setup. The unnecessary errors that have to be reduced in number are the kind in which you make a mistake for no apparent reason. Here are some examples: you hit a groundstroke into the net or out of bounds while your opponent is in a backcourt position; you fail to return an easy second serve; you double fault; you overhit a smash at the net.

Reducing the number of unforced errors also means taking no needless risks. You should not try "quarter shots" when "nickel shots" will win the point. If a three-quarter speed serve deep to the backhand will probably win the point or lead to winning the point, why go for the ace? If a shot that hits 3 feet inside a line will win a point, why try to hit closer to the line? If a crisp crosscourt volley wins, why attempt a drop shot? If difficult shots must be attempted, at least learn when to try them. Nonpercentage shots should not be tried unless you are in a desperate situation during a point or unless you are in a comfortable lead in a game or set. Even then, the low-percentage shot can be dangerous. The momentum in a match can change with one shot. Many 40-0 games and some 5-0 sets have been lost by the person who had the big lead.

There are specific shots to be hit in playing low-risk, percentage tennis. Here are some of them:

1.   Groundstrokes hit from the baseline should usually be hit crosscourt. The distance from corner to corner is greater than from middle to middle, so you will have more space to work with. The net is lower at the middle than at the side, and crosscourt shots will travel over the middle of the net. Crosscourt groundstrokes make your opponents run more and consequently tire more quickly than if you give them the luxury of returning balls hit down the middle. Crosscourt groundstrokes stay in the air longer, so you can follow your shot to the net or can have more time to anticipate where the return shot will be hit. Finally, crosscourt shots do not travel close to the alleys, so there is less chance that a mis-hit ball will go out of bounds on the side.

2. Groundstrokes should not only be hit crosscourt, they should also be hit deep into the backcourt of your opponent. Hitting too deep may be considered a low-percentage shot from the standpoint of keeping the ball in play, but the deep shot reduces the opportunity of the opponent to hit an attacking shot on the return. The longer your opponent stays on or behind the baseline, the more time you have to set him or her up for a forced error or a winning shot.

3. To hit deep into the backcourt, you should hit the ball high over the net, assuming that your opponent is not in a position to volley. Hitting high over the net gives you a safer margin of error in respect to netting the ball, keeps opponent away from the net, and makes him or her play shots with half volleys. A shot that clears the net by several feet also gives you time to rush behind your groundstroke.

4. Approach shots should usually be hit down the line unless your opponent is especially vulnerable to shots hit directly at him or her. The down-the-line shot should enable you to establish a position at the net so that you can cut off the return. Your opponent can either return the shot down the same line or go down the middle. You should be in a position to hit a put-away volley on either shot. It is almost impossible for your opponent to hit a crosscourt shot off of the deep, down-the-line approach shot; the only other alternative is the lob, but you will also be in a good position to hit the overhead smash. It is important that the down-the-line approach shot be hit deeply, especially on slow courts. If the shot falls short, your opponent can advance into the ball and hit a passing shot. The approach shot should be hit with backspin on the backhand side, but may be hit with topspin, backspin, or even sidespin on the forehand side.

5. Volleys should be hit to the open spot on the court or to the opponent's weakness. Just as football players "run to daylight," tennis players should automatically hit where the opponent is not. This usually means hitting crosscourt. There are exceptions, such as when your opponent is anticipating the crosscourt volley and has already started to move in the right direction. Then the volley may be hit down the line or down the middle in anticipation of where the open spot will be. Remember that the crosscourt volley does not have to hit near the line to be a winner. If the first volley is not good enough to be a winning shot, the second volley should be. If you stay at the net more than three consecutive volleys, the odds on your winning the point diminish considerably.

6. First serves should be placed to the outside of the service court in order to force the receiver off the court. That means that your serves will be hit to the receiver's forehand half the time, but if the serve is placed deeply enough or angled sharply enough, the effect of the forehand

return will be lessened. The secondary target for first serves is the receiver's backhand, assuming that your opponent's backhand is weaker than the forehand. That is not always true, however, especially among advanced players. On the left side of the court, both purposes will be served (hitting to the backhand and pulling the receiver off the court) if the ball is placed to the outside of the service court. Even if the first and second choices of targets are dictated by percentages, you can still utilize the strategy of mixing up serves in regard to placement, velocity, spin, and capability of the receiver. There are times when variety of attack is just as effective as hitting the textbook shot.

7.   Second serves should be hit in, with more topspin than the first serve, and as deeply as possible without risking a double fault. Hitting the ball inside the service court boundaries—keeping the ball in play—is more important than any other consideration. Percentages do not mean anything if the ball is never put into play. Putting topspin on the second serve makes it possible to serve the ball high over the net and at the same time forces the ball to drop in a more vertical trajectory than the first serve. Both actions result in a safer serve. Putting topspin on the second serve also makes the ball bounce higher, requiring an adjustment by the receiver. Hitting deeply should keep the receiver from hitting an attacking shot on the return.

8.   Lobs should be hit to your opponent's backhand side when possible. The high backhand is one of tennis's most difficult shots to handle. If the opponent hits it, the shot cannot have much power. If the player runs around the ball so it can be hit with a normal overhead smash, you will have time to defend against it.

In playing low-risk tennis, you should avoid going for winners (point-ending shots) in certain situations:

1.   Winners should not be attempted on serves. The odds on hitting aces are slim. The well-placed first serve with moderate speed will win the point for you more than half of the time. The winning shot usually comes on the second or third ball played after the serve. The player who goes for the ace throughout the match will wear out sooner, especially on slow courts and in hot weather.

2.   Winners should not be attempted on approach shots. The idea is to hit the ball deeply and down the line, not to put the ball away. The put-away follows the good approach shot.

3.   Winners should not be attempted on the first groundstroke passing shot. When your opponent has rushed the net, the first shot at him or

her should be low, firmly hit, and directed at the player's weakest side. The winning shot should come on your next return because net players cannot do much with a volley on which they have to hit up.

4. Winners should not be attempted on overhead smashes from a position in the backcourt. The opponent has too much time to scramble for a return, the distance is too long to put good pace on the ball, your angle for hitting is poor, and the ball stays in the air so long that your opponent has time to set up the next shot.

5. Winners should not be attempted by hitting drop shots from a position in the backcourt. Again, the ball stays in the air so long that your opponent has time to get to it and perhaps put it away. It is also a low-percentage shot because it may be netted.

Playing Against Different Styles

An inherent problem in tennis is that players usually practice against the same group of players and learn all of their strengths and weaknesses because they see them so often. In a tournament or match these players have to adjust to a new style within a few minutes. For many players, by the time that adjustment is made, the match is almost over. There is no advice that can completely solve this problem, but there are things that the intermediate and even advanced players can do to counteract specific styles among tennis players. You can make these adjustments if you are competent enough to make changes and observant enough to recognize a style of play when you see it.

First, consider the big hitters. They probably have a heavy, hard, flat serve, blistering groundstrokes, put-away volleys, and the big overhead smash. They like to serve and rush the net. Their asset is power. Their weaknesses may be (but not always) lack of patience, poor mobility, and inconsistency. It is difficult to consistently move and hit big shots for very long. You are going to have to learn to take advantage of these weaknesses.

What can you do about the big serve? You can play a step or two deeper on the return, if necessary. You can block or chip the serve and try to return it low and at your opponent's feet. Big hitters are frequently big people, and it is harder for them to bend their knees to get down on the low volley than for smaller players. In blocking or chipping the big serve, take a short backswing, hold your racket tightly, and use the pace provided by the server. The harder the serve is hit, the more you can act as a backboard with your racket to reflect the power shots. If you can get the first serve back in play, the big hitter has lost one of his best weapons. He may also lose his patience later in the match.

What can you do to counteract the heavily hit groundstrokes? Again, use the pace provided by the stronger hitter rather than trying to overpower the power hitter. As much as possible, your returns should force the big hitter to run, hit on the run, bend, stretch, and work hard. All of this should have a cumulative effect of weakening these players' power shots. They want to hit a few hard shots and blow you off the court. You want to keep them on the court and moving as long as possible. The longer they are on the court, the less consistent and less powerful their big shots should become.

To cope with the strong volleys, make the heavy hitters reach for balls. Make them prove their overhead smash again and again. They will make you look bad on some points, but if that stroke is not solid or if they are not in shape, the smash will fall apart later in the match. Make them bend down to hit volleys. Nobody can do much with a low shot at the net. The big hitters will still go for the winner, but their margin of error is small. They could use the drop shot, but big hitters sometimes consider that shot beneath their dignity.

If the big hitter is a superior player, no amount of strategy is going to help you win the match. If you have some weapons of your own, the big hitting player can be beaten. Slugging matches with this player should be avoided by keeping the ball in play, keeping it low, and moving the ball around the court as much as possible.

Some tennis players build their games around the big, topspin forehand shot. It can be devastating, as Rod Laver, Tom Okker, Bjorn Borg, and other well-known players have proven. There are ways to minimize the topspinner's attack, but it is not easy.

One tactic, if you can call it that, is to avoid playing this kind of opponent on a slow surface. The extreme topspin requires either a big windup or a quick wrist, and slow courts give the player who uses the topspin time to prepare for the shot. Fast courts do not; they make the ball slide by before the windup is complete or before the wrist comes over the top of the ball. Even though you may not be able to choose the kind of surface you play on, this information may give you a psychological boost when you play a topspinner on a fast court. You may be depressed if you have to play the same type on a slower court.

A second suggestion is to keep the ball deep. This advice is true for almost any kind of player, but it is a must to keep the topspinner from charging, teeing off with the looping shot, and following it to the net. The deep shot forces the player making the return to retreat and to give up some of the forward motion necessary to execute the topspin groundstroke. The topspinner's only other alternative is to attempt a topspin shot off of the short hop, which is a low-percentage shot.

In addition to keeping the ball deep, you should play the ball to the backhand side of opponents who use the topspin forehand. Placing the ball anywhere but on their strong side is good advice. Occasionally, they will try to run around their backhand to hit the ball with a forehand. If that happens, they will leave an open spot for you to shoot at on the return.

To counteract the action of a topspin shot that bounces near your baseline, you must strike the ball while it is on the rise. Otherwise, your groundstroke will be hit about head high, so it will be a weaker shot from the backcourt, or you will have to hit the ball as it descends. Against the good topspin, this means you might have to retreat well behind the baseline to hit a groundstroke. From that position it is difficult to hit anything but defensive shots.

The retrievers or pushers present a different set of problems. They attempt to get everything back, are masters at keeping the ball in play, and do not try to overpower you. But the retrievers also have weaknesses, and here are some ways to take advantage of them.

Retrievers have to be moved up and back—from the baseline to the net and back again. Pushers are not usually strong net players, so they should be brought to the net. To get them there, challenge their ability to hit a strong approach shot. A moderately short groundstroke to either side will force the pusher to come forward. If the player does not put the approach shot away or back you into a corner, he or she is probably stuck at the net or in midcourt and may be set up for a passing shot or a lob. If your opponent gets out of that jam, repeat the tactic during the same rally, if you can.

Another possible tactic to use against pushers is to occasionally over-power them. It is important not to become impatient against these players by trying to outpower them more than occasionally. Their specialty is getting shots back, and some would-be put-aways will come back. Power mixed with short shots, deep groundstrokes, and forcing returns on your opponent's second serve can be very effective. Anything that will keep them off balance and out of their groove will diminish their chances of winning. The one thing to avoid is playing the pusher's game. They are better at it, conditioned to be on the courts for a long time, and patient enough to let you beat yourself.

Playing against lefthanders is a special problem for most players— even lefthanded ones. What can you do to get ready to fight a southpaw? The first step is to learn the general characteristics of the lefthanded player. The obvious advantage of the lefties lies in their groundstrokes. Their shots are not that different from those of other players, but opponents grooved to hit to the backhand find themselves hitting into a forehand. The lefthanders know this and can anticipate what is about to happen. By deliberately leaving you a little daylight on their forehand side, they can really entice you into hitting to their strength. The player who makes a conscious effort can probably adjust to the lefthander at the beginning of points and during low-pressure points. But at a crucial moment, it is easy to forget and revert to your grooved strokes—right into your opponent's forehand. Only intense concentration throughout the match can help you avoid this problem.

Lefthanders have an even greater advantage on their serve. Most players are not accustomed to the spin produced by a lefthanded serve, which makes the ball bounce to the receiver's left instead of the right. Some players take the entire match just to figure out the spin and bounce. Practice in returning your opponent's warmup serves may partially solve this problem.

The lefthander's serve from the left court also presents a unique problem to you if you are righthanded. If the lefthander can serve to the outside of the service court with a spin serve, the combination of trajectory and spin will force you into or beyond the alley for the service return. You also have to make the return with your backhand, which is probably not your strongest shot. Lefties who follow their serve to the net can cheat to their right because of the probable angle of return. The ball will probably be returned down the line or down the middle; either way, the server has a wide open court in which to hit the follow-up volley. You can reduce this advantage by stepping forward rather than laterally to your left on the return, cutting the ball off before it draws you too far away from the court.

A third characteristic of lefthanded players is an apparent preference for hitting the oversmash to their left side instead of coming across their body to their right, which should be a more natural motion. No one, not even the lefthander, has explained this wrong side syndrome. He or she may admit a preference, but may not be able to give you a reason for it. The righthander can be prepared for the reverse action smash by anticipating it and moving to the right as the ball is hit.[2]

Playing on Various Surfaces

The type of court you play on should be considered when developing singles or doubles strategy. There are too many synthetic surfaces for an analysis of each one. Even with one type of court composition there may be a wide range. Concrete courts, for example, can be very slow or very slick. Generally, courts are either fast, slow, or in between, and you can make adjustments for at least two of these three.

[2] Jim Brown, "Thinking Lefthanded," *Scholastic Coach*, 42, no. 7 (March 1973), 68.

If you are going to play a match on a fast surface, make these adjustments in planning your strategy and in stroke production:

1. Get your racket back sooner and start your swing earlier than on slower surfaces. The ball will bounce low and fast, and will tend to slide by you unless the racket is brought forward sooner. A shorter backswing than usual may be necessary in order to meet the ball in time and in front of the body.

2. Play deeper than usual, especially on the service return. The extra step or two back in the court will give you another fraction of a second to get ready and hit.

3. You can attack on shots that would not be attacking shots on slower surfaces. A better than average serve, volley, or approach shot becomes a great shot if the surface is fast enough. You can be more aggressive if you can handle the serve and groundstrokes of your opponent.

4. For the reasons just stated, you can expect your opponent to be more aggressive on these courts than on slow courts. You may have to defend against the serve and rush style of play against players who would not normally play that way.

5. You will probably be able to play longer matches or longer periods of time without tiring as much as you would on other courts. Fast courts tend to produce short exchanges on many points, so you can expect to do less running. If you know you are going to be on the court for a shorter period of time, you may be able to play at a more intense pace during the match.

6. Be especially conscious of staying down low on groundstrokes. Since the ball will slide more and bounce up less, you must bend your knees and stay down there with the ball.

For competition on slow surfaces, the following changes in style and tactics might be effective:

1. You will have more time to prepare for shots. Be more deliberate, wait longer to make a decision about where to hit the ball, and do not give up on retrieving shots you would not normally be able to reach.

2. On slow courts, be patient. It takes more time to beat somebody because the ball stays in play longer. The player who wants to get things over with in a hurry will become frustrated on these courts. This is a weakness that you should take advantage of if you do not mind taking your time.

3. Do not wear yourself out trying to hit the big serve when playing on these surfaces. The ball is going to bite and slow down when it bounces, so the steam will go out of the hard-hit serve. It is better for you to pace yourself for a longer match and to save your big serve for special situations.

4. Also consider using a serve with more spin than you would use on fast courts. Because the ball bites into the surface, the effect of the spin will be greater.

5. Be very careful about advancing to the net when you play on slow courts. Even professional players are reluctant to follow a serve on clay courts, Rubico courts, and some of the slower synthetic surfaces. Approach shots have to be expertly placed before you follow the ball into the forecourt. Shallow serves and short approaches turn offensive tactics into positions of defense.

6. If you have developed the strokes, you may be able to use top-spin groundstrokes more frequently on slower courts. There is more time to set up and to bring the racket head up to the ball. At the same time, be prepared to defend against that shot in case your opponent has the same idea.

7. Do not underestimate the pusher or retriever on these courts. They are made for this player's game. Players who look slow, weak, and easy to beat on fast courts may be fast enough, strong enough, and tough enough to win on their own kind of court.

8. If you know you are going to play most of your tournaments or matches on slow courts, be more conscientious about your physical condition. You are going to be out there a long time—win or lose.

There is no special advice that can be given for play on "in-between" court surfaces. Each person decides for himself or herself what is fast or slow and must adjust accordingly. For the player with fast reflex reactions, a strong forearm, and a short backswing, the medium fast surface may play the same as a slow court would for other players. Whatever the surface, the best strategy is to try to arrange to practice on it before having to play a match. If you lose, do not blame it on the surface; good players win on slow, medium, and fast courts.

Adjusting to the Elements

Fair weather tennis players complain about the wind, sun, and the heat. They stall, look disgusted, do not enjoy themselves, and frequently lose. Tennis is not as enjoyable when the weather is not perfect, but all players have to play in less than perfect conditions sooner or later, so it makes sense to learn how to cope with the elements rather than to lose to them. When the wind is a factor, consider these suggestions:

1.   Toss the ball lower than usual on the serve. Lowering the toss reduces the margin of error because the ball tends to move with the wind on a higher toss, causing you to have to make a last-second adjustment in your service motion.

2.   Do not attempt drop shots when the wind is at your back. The wind can turn what would normally be a winning drop shot into a floater which your opponent has time to reach and possibly put away.

3.   Keep lobbing to a minimum. It is simply too risky on a windy day, especially if the wind is gusting. If you must lob, use a highly arched defensive lob when you are with the wind, and a harder, lower lob against the wind. If the wind is with you, try to have a trajectory that peaks over the top of the net. If the wind is against you, aim the ball so that its highest point in flight will pass over the opponent's service line.

4.   When with the wind, play a step or two closer to the net in most situations (especially on the service return). When you are against the wind, play slightly deeper than usual. One exception is when you are serving with a strong wind at your back. If your serve tends to go deep, try standing a step behind the baseline. The added distance might compensate for the extra push the wind gives your serve.

5.   Take more chances when you are playing against the wind. Shots that would normally be too high, too hard, or too deep often become well-hit shots against the wind. You cannot play a normal groundstroke game against the wind. You must force the action or be blown off the court by your opponent or the wind.

6.   Conversely, play more conservatively with the wind. Shots that would usually be safe placements become winners when the extra pace is provided by the wind.

7.   When playing doubles on a windy day, let the partner with the more powerful serve go against the wind while the weaker server uses the wind to make his or her serve stronger. If there is no difference between the two players, let the partner who is weaker at the net play that position when the other partner serves with the wind. This forces the opponents to return serves against the wind, slowing the ball, and giving the weaker net player more time to react.

8.   Before the match begins, consider using your alternative on the racket spin to play against the wind during the first game. Even if your

opponent wins that serve, you will change after the first game and then have the wind at your back for two consecutive games.

Here are some factors to think about when looking into the sun during a match:

1.   When serving, toss the ball farther to either side of your head than usual, or toss the ball behind your head to avoid looking into the sun. When either of these variations is used, the ball must be served with an unusual amount of spin. Although both serves may be effective, serves with spin will have less velocity than flatter serves. This means your opponent has more time to react to your serve, but it also gives you more time to establish a position if you rush the net.

2.   If you are playing against the sun and depend on a serve and volley game, consider the fact that any lob your opponent hits is going to force you to look into the sun. On the other hand, if your opponent comes to the net, give him more than the usual quota of lobs when he is on the sunny side. He is trying to gain an advantage by cutting down the size of the court, so there is nothing unethical about making him pay for his aggressive behavior.

3.   In doubles, two righthanders may have varying service styles, so that one is less affected by playing the sun court than the other. This factor should be considered at the beginning of the match when the order of serving is established for the first set. If a lefthander and righthander play together, you can arrange a rotation so that neither player has to be bothered by looking into the sun while serving.

Although the temperature and humidity create obvious problems, many tournament players disregard both factors until it is too late. The price they pay is a lost match or a less effective performance in subsequent matches. Generally, the bigger a player's game, the more likely he or she is to wilt under the heat of the sun. It is very difficult for some people to learn to pace themselves, but these ideas might help:

1.   Be careful about using a maximum velocity serve during the first set. While the big serve might win some early battles, it takes so much out of you that the war might be lost later. A big server who does not win a match in two sets will probably be in trouble in the third.

2.   Select some times during a game to serve and stay in the back-court. Points can be won without serving and rushing. It is very demanding for a player to serve and rush the net fifty times in one set even under

normal conditions. The longer the match lasts, the more fatigued you will become, the less you will advance toward the net, and the weaker your volleys will be. Put them all together and you lose in three sets.

3. Although it is easier said than done, make your opponent move around the court. Now is not the time to blast him off the court, but rather to run him so much that he leaves voluntarily.

4. Keep the racket handle dry. There are several ways that can be done: using commercial products that are sprayed or rubbed onto the grip; keeping hand towels close by; alternating wrist bands throughout the match; changing rackets every two or three games; putting sawdust in your pocket and using it as a drying agent; wrapping adhesive gauze to the handle; and carrying the racket in the nonracket hand between points (which not only helps to keep the handle dry, but also reduces fatigue in the muscles of the racket hand and forearm).

5. Dress comfortably and coolly. Loosely fitting clothes give your skin a chance to breathe. Lighter colored clothes reflect the sun's rays whereas darker colors absorb the heat. Have at least one extra shirt at the courtside. Change shirts during a break, if it is practical to do so.

6. Stay in the shade as much as possible between points and games. Just those few seconds out of the direct sunlight can give you a boost.

7. Go to the courts with a supply of water, and drink it frequently. Do not try to show that you are tough by going an entire set or match without drinking anything. The fluid you lose during a match needs to be replaced quickly, not after the match is over.

8. Wear a hat. It will keep hair out of your eyes and perspiration from running down your face. It will also provide a little shade and prevent you from being overexposed to the sun.

No suggestion is going to enable a weak player to beat a stronger player. But if everything else is equal, knowing how to play in all kinds of weather can give you an advantage.

Avoiding Tactical Errors

Beginning and intermediate players frequently lose matches because of relatively simple errors. Ironically, many tactical errors are made when these players attempt to imitate better, more experienced players. There is nothing wrong with watching superior players and trying to pattern part of your game after theirs. However, the average recreational or weekend player does not have the strength, speed, agility, or background of the world's best players. Therefore, it makes sense for lesser players to adjust their playing strategies to be consistent with their talent. Although it would be difficult to define and comment on every possible tactical error made by the beginning or intermediate player, here are some problems to avoid:

1. *Blasting the first serve.* The first serve is probably the most abused offensive weapon in tennis. Too many inexperienced players try to knock their opponents off the court with the first serve, then follow it with a very weak second serve. Very few good players hit their first serves as hard as they can. Most use a combination of power and spin, with more power on the first serve and more spin on the second.

Use two three-quarter speed serves rather than one bomb and one nothing serve. A well-placed off-speed serve to your opponent's backhand or to an open spot in the service court is just as effective as the attempted ace. The percentages say that your opponent will not return the serve or that it will be returned so weakly that your next shot can be put away for a winner. Once the three-quarter serve has been mastered, adding a wrist rotation at the peak of the service motion can produce a power serve that will be more than adequate. It should be used sparingly—just often enough to keep your opponent honest.

2. *Rushing the net at the wrong time.* Many inexperienced players use a suicide strategy in charging the net. For apparently self-sacrificial reasons, they rush forward during a point courageously, but futilely. Others try to sneak up to the net as if to surprise their opponents (following a weak second serve, for example). The opponent will certainly be surprised, and very pleasantly so, because it is easy to hit a passing shot against this kind of player.

Do not rush the net at all unless you can handle shots in the forecourt area. If you can play at the net, rush only when your opponent is at a disadvantage—for example, after you have hit a shot deep to the backhand, pulling your opponent off to one side of the court, or after you have lobbed over your opponent's head. The only time your opponent should be surprised is upon turning around after chasing down a well-placed, angled, deep shot, and seeing you at the net ready for a put-away volley or overhead smash.

3. *Spectating.* Some players should pay admission to their own matches. They frequently seem to be surprised when a shot comes at them. The reasons could be lack of concentration, laziness, or just plain admiration of their own last shot. Whatever the reasons, the results are disastrous.

Expect every ball to come back at you, regardless of how hard the previous shot was hit or how well placed. Get back to a central position after every shot. By observing your opponent in various situations, you can learn to anticipate what is likely to happen on the next shot.

You can learn a lot by watching good baseball infielders and out-fielders just before a pitch. Although the odds are low on any one pitch being hit to one of the seven fielders, each player crouches, stays up on the toes, and springs forward on each pitch. They expect each ball to be hit directly to them. In tennis, the odds are at least even that every shot you hit is going to come back at you. Be ready to hit it.

4. *Playing too far from the net.* Many players seem to think that by not crowding the net, they are improving their chances for a return. Some are afraid to get too close to the net for fear of being hit, and others are afraid of being passed.

The farther back from the net you stand, the greater the margin of error on volleys. Standing too far back can result in shots that dribble off the racket and into the net, and it gives your opponent more time to react to the volley when the shot does clear the net. World class players stand in the area near the service line, but remember that their skills are vastly different from yours.

Start out standing a racket's length and a couple of steps from the net. Once you feel comfortable at that distance, move back to a position in which you can cover more territory. Until you reach that level, it is better to stay close to the net. You will lose some points because of passing shots and lobs, but you will win others because of a better attacking position and a better position from which to deflect shots that would not have made it over the net from a position farther back in the court.

5. *Playing the big game.* Aspiring players watch the great players for pointers. However, many established players are using a serve, rush, and volley type of game which most people cannot play effectively. When they attempt the same kind of strategy, a tragedy of errors usually follows. At most levels, points, games, sets, and matches are lost rather than won. Most intermediates who rely on big shots to win, will not.

Keep the ball in play. This does not mean just pushing the ball back, but using sound, crisp groundstrokes mixed occasionally with the big shots. Tennis games should be built from the baseline forward. Develop a reliable serve, forehand, and backhand before trying too many volleys, smashes, and other put-away shots. A solid game from the baseline will force your opponent into game-losing errors and set you up for game-winning big shots as a match progresses.

6. *Trying to look good rather than playing to win.* This problem is closely related to playing the big game. Too many players feel that if you do not play the big game, you are pushing, and pushing is a dirty word in

tennis circles. Others do not seem to care whether they win or lose, but only how they look to the crowd. These players are noted for looking sensational during the warmup, but falling apart once the match begins. To add to the problem, they keep convincing themselves that their game is just "off" when they lose. To be more accurate, their true game is "off" when they win, which is seldom.

If you are serious about tennis, play to win. Forget what the books say about clothes, a lot of tennis etiquette, and how the pros play the game. Within the bounds of efficient form, good players develop their own styles of hitting. Most of the top players of the world have peculiarities about their games not found in tennis textbooks. Yet, these men and women have reached the top because they use the form that suits their size, strength, quickness, and philosophy of tennis. If pushing wins, push. If scrambling wins, scramble. If hitting a two-handed backhand wins, do it. If just looking good on the court is not enough to win, forget about looking good.[3]

Strategy—Point by Point

As you gradually develop the ability to utilize plans and strategies in your game, you may want to give some thought to playing each point or game according to percentages. The idea that some points in a game, set, or match are more important than others is not new, but to plan strategy accordingly requires a relatively sophisticated game. For beginners, adjusting your game plan on a point-by-point basis is impossible. For intermediate players, it is something to consider, but should not be the determining factor in how you play a match.

Here are a few thoughts on important points and games. Generally, the closer the score, the greater your effort should be to avoid unnecessary errors. For example, when the score is 30-30, deuce, or either player's advantage, that is not the time to be taking chances on low-percentage shots or to play on the outer edge of your ability. You are in the game, you have a good chance to win the game, and you do not want to take a chance on losing by trying very difficult shots. Do not revert to merely punching the ball across the net, but hit shots firmly while giving your opponent at least an equal chance to make an error. The same strategy applies when you are tied in games, especially late in a set. Play percentage tennis to the letter by (1) getting your first serve in play, (2) hitting crosscourt groundstrokes when your opponent is on his or her baseline, (3) hitting down-the-line approach shots, (4) volleying to the

---

[3] Jim Brown, "Seven Cardinal Sins of High School Tennis Players," *Scholastic Coach*, 41, no. 7 (March 1972), 68.

open spot, (5) lobbing to the backhand, and (6) waiting for the right time to go for the winner.

The time to be a bit more aggressive or to try those big shots that you really want to get out of your system is when you are far ahead or far behind. If you are ahead 40-0 or 40-15 in a game, or ahead by several games in a set, you should be relaxed and confident enough to play up to your maximum ability. If you lose a point because you attempt a difficult shot, you are still in good shape to close out the game on the next point. The pressure is on your opponent, who knows one mistake will end the game. Do not try absolutely wild shots, but you can use your big advantage in the score to put more variety in your shots.

If you are behind at 30-0, 40-15, or 40-0, you might as well be bolder to get back into the game. Chances are that your opponent will be playing more loosely than usual, so it will probably take a good shot or at least an aggressive shot to pick up a point. If you lose the point, it may be some consolation to know that you probably would have lost the game anyway. If, by playing more aggressively, you win a point and get back into the game, tighten up your strokes on subsequent points. In the context of a set, if you are ahead by a substantial margin, keep the pressure on. If you are losing big, try something different to make the set closer.

If there is one point in a game that is more decisive than others, it is probably the fourth point when the score is 30-15 or 15-30. If you are ahead and win the next point, you will have the game well in control. If you are behind and win the fourth point, it is a new game. What can you do about playing this point? Give an extra effort, concentrate harder, and make sure you do not hit to your opponent's strength.

The most important game in a set may be the seventh game when the score is 4-2 or 2-4. If you are leading and pick up the seventh game, the 5-2 gap is almost impossible to close. If you are behind 4-2, winning the seventh game puts you right back into a competitive position, especially if you will be serving the eighth game. If you are pacing yourself in the set, do not hold back during the 4-2 or 2-4 seventh game. Play it at full speed. It will be worth the extra energy you spend.

There are two other possible turning points in tennis. As an intermediate player, you should be holding your serve more often than losing it. The same thing applies to your opponent. The best time to break a serve is following a service break. If you lose your serve, be ready to get that game back by really jumping on your opponent on the first points of the next game. He or she may relax a bit after having worked hard to beat you on your serve. If so, take advantage of the situation. Conversely, if you win your opponent's serve, be aware that the other player may be thinking the same thing.

If you lose a set, concentrate on winning the first two games at the beginning of the next set. There is a natural tendency in most players to relax after winning a set, especially the first set, because they know they have a cushion to rest on for a while. If your opponent lets down, put on the pressure before he or she has time to recover.

Putting Your Plans Together

Developing singles strategy will ultimately come down to what you can do best. If you are a pusher at heart, all the strategy in the world will not help you change your style or strategy. If you are determined to try big shots throughout a match, it's your game. Discussions about percentages, different styles, various surfaces, elements, and important game situations are important only in retrospect if you cannot or will not do anything differently. Do not be too discouraged if this is where your game is right now. Most intermediates and many advanced players are not capable of adjusting their strategy as a game or set progresses. In that case, the only important point is the next one.

DOUBLES

Positioning

Many tennis books promote the idea that there is only one way to play doubles, and that is for the partners to play parallel to each other on the court most of the time and to get to the net at the first opportunity. If both players have the skills to play that style of game, then they should stay together and get to the net. But many players cannot play so aggressively or expertly, and that same strategy for them will be disastrous. It makes no sense to serve and rush if you cannot handle yourself in the forecourt. If you are good at the net and your partner is more comfortable in a backcourt position, play the up and back strategy. You have plenty of time to develop your skills to the point of playing the more classic style of doubles.

Here are some possible alignments for beginning and intermediate doubles play. If you are the server, you should stand halfway between the middle of the baseline and the doubles sideline. From this position you can cover the court from the center line to the alley on your side. Your partner should stand on the opposite side of the court about a racket's length and two steps from the net and approximately one step away from the alley toward the center of the court. From this position your partner can cut off shots hit to his or her side of the court on the service return and throughout the point. The player at the net should leave just enough daylight in the alley for the person returning the serve to be tempted to try a passing shot. After you serve, you defend your side of the court from the baseline and the net player defends his or her side from the forecourt position. If the return of serve is lobbed over the player at the net, you should cross over to return the lob while the net player moves over to play the other side of the court. If the net player poaches to cut off a return, you must move to cover the part of the court left open. If the point does not end with the attempted poach, the net player must take a position on one side of the court rather than staying in the middle. Then you will know which side of the court to defend from the backcourt. More about poaching later.

If you are the service receiver, you should stand in front of, on, or slightly behind the baseline, depending on how fast the server is hitting the ball. Stand directly in line with the expected path of the ball, which is usually very near the alley. If you are a beginner, concentrate on returning the serve and do not worry about rushing the net after your return. If you can play the net, and if your return is a well-placed crosscourt shot, follow the shot to a volleying position in the forecourt on your side. If the return is not that good, wait for a deep shot before you go to the net. If your partner can play well at the net, he or she should begin the point stationed on the service line halfway between the middle of the court and the singles sideline. If your return of the serve is either angled sharply or placed deeply, your partner should advance to the net and defend his or her side of the court from a volleying position. If your partner is not effective at the net, he or she should begin the point back on the baseline even with you. As the point is played, your partner should maintain that position while you wait for an opportunity to move to the net. If both of you are weak at the net, you should both stay on the baseline, at least while the other team is serving. Figures 61 and 62 illustrate how beginning and intermediate doubles might line up to begin a point.

Poaching

Poaching is a tactic used in doubles in which the player at the net cuts across in front of the partner to volley a shot that would normally have gone to the backcourt. It is not something for beginners to be trying, but intermediate players should know why to do it, how to do it, and when to do it. When the poach is used wisely, it can be a deadly and demoralizing shot. When it is overused or used at the wrong time, it can get you in more trouble than it is worth.

The most obvious answer to the question, "Why poach?" is: to win a point. It is a good way to win a point, and it is especially effective against a person who is having trouble returning the serve. A person who has to give full attention to just getting the ball back cannot be wondering what the player at the net is going to do. That gives the net player quite a bit of freedom to poach. Another reason to use the poach occasionally is to keep the opponent off balance. The threat of a poach may be as effective as the put-away volley itself. The tactic just gives your opponent one more thing to worry about.

The poach is usually a running volley. If you decide to poach, move with your racket back in a short backswing position. Move in a way so that you can advance toward the ball as you hit rather than moving laterally. The forward motion will add zip to your punch volley. Find out which is the better side for you to poach from. Most players can stretch farther on the forehand side than on the backhand, so they should do most of their poaching when they move toward the ball with their forehand. Hit the

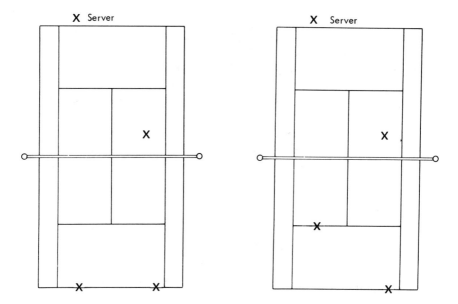

Figure 61 (left). Here are the positions for beginning doubles players prior to the serve. The position of the receiver's partner could change, depending on ability to play at the net, how good the server is, and how good the receiver is at returning serves. Until you know the answers to those questions, line up like this.

Figure 62 (right). Intermediate level doubles players line up the same as beginners with the exception that the receiver's partner usually begins on the service line. He can adjust his position if the receiver has trouble in returning the serve. After the service return, the receiver's partner must either advance closer to the net or fall back to the baseline.

ball between your opponents or at the feet of the one closer to the net. Move to one side of the court after your volley. You cannot play the middle and expect your partner to cover both sides.

When to poach may be the most important question. First, do not poach in high-risk situations, that is, when the set or match may be riding on one shot and when your team may be in trouble already. Do your poaching when (1) your opponents are not expecting a poach, (2) a weak opponent is returning a serve or groundstroke, (3) your partner hits deep or hard-to-return serves or groundstrokes, and (4) you are absolutely sure you want to poach. Half-hearted poaches are worse than no poaches at all.

Selecting Partners

The most important factor in developing a good doubles team is deciding who to play with. Good singles players are not necessarily good doubles players, so do not assume that the player at the top of the challenge ladder will automatically be a champion doubles player. Find someone to play with who you can get along with on and off the court. Do not choose someone who will criticize you after a bad shot or who you might do the same thing to. If you like someone, you should be able to communicate with that person on the court by talking, looking, moving, reassuring, anticipating, and shot making. Your communication can be verbal or nonverbal. Each method is not only acceptable, but desirable. Doubles is truly a team effort, and without cooperation, patience, and understanding, a team has little chance of success, even if both players are talented.

A second consideration in choosing a partner is style of play. Doubles partners must have games that complement each other. A power player should usually team up with a steady player. With this combination, one player can take the aggressive role and the other can see that the ball is kept in play long enough to have a chance at winning the point. If two big hitters play together, they are either very good or very bad. When two retrievers play on the same doubles team, they have trouble putting opponents away.

Each partner must accept his or her role as part of the doubles team. The steady player must accept the fact that the partner is going to take more chances, hit more winners, and probably make more mistakes. If both players are going for big shots and taking chances, a hole is frequently left open somewhere on the court. Aggressive partners must be disciplined enough to know when to go for big shots and patient enough to give their partners a chance to set them up for the winner. A few players have the ability to be aggressive or to be consistent, depending on the partner's style of play. If you can develop that kind of game, you will be in demand as a doubles partner.

Another factor in determining doubles teams involves playing with a righthander or lefthander. If two righthanders play together, the player with the stronger backhand should play the left court. This player's backhand will be needed for the return of serves to the outside of the odd (left) court. If two lefthanders play together, the player with the better backhand should play the deuce (right) court for the same reason. The situation is exactly the same, but on the other side of the court. If a righthander and lefthander play together, the righthander should play the right side and the lefthander the left side. They may be weak down the middle where their backhands are, but the benefits of having the forehand crosscourt service returns outweigh the risks.

Low-Risk Doubles

There are certain shots that should be hit in doubles. Here are some of them:

1.   First serves should be placed to the outside of the service court, to the receiver's backhand, to an open spot, or occasionally right into the receiver. If that sounds ambiguous, it is because there are too many variables to say absolutely that "this is where you should serve the ball in doubles." Each target has advantages and disadvantages. Serving to the outside pulls the receiver off the court and reduces the angle of return. Against righthanders playing the right side of the court, the outside serve will go to your opponent's forehand, which may be his or her strong shot. Serving to the backhand is usually good percentage tennis, but in some cases your opponent will hit a backhand from the middle of the court, thus having a good chance for a well-placed return. Hitting to the open spot is a good idea except when your opponent has deliberately left you a little room, hoping you will hit to his or her strength. Some players have trouble handling serves hit directly at them, especially if they are expecting the wide serve.

2.   Second serves should be hit inside the service court. If that sounds too simple, it is because there is no excuse for double faulting in doubles. You (the server) have to cover only half the court, so you can be more conservative. Serving with topspin will allow you to serve higher over the net and still get the ball into the court. Flat and twist serves are riskier.

3.   Beginners and intermediates should return serves high over the net, crosscourt, and deep (if the server does not rush the net).

4. As mentioned earlier, a player at the net who poaches on the return of serve should hit either between the opponents or at the feet of the receiver's partner. This is the safest, most effective place to hit. Hitting at an opponent to attempt to win a point is not unethical tennis.

5. When poaching, keep drop shots and severe angles to a minimum. They are spectacular shots, but they do not win as many points as volleys directed at or through your opponents.

6. After the serve and return of serve, most shots should be hit down the middle and low. Hitting to the middle can cause confusion about which player will take the shot and draws both players in, leaving more open space for put-aways.

7. On shots hit down the middle, the player with the forehand shot should make the return. The forehand is usually the stronger shot, and having a predetermined system will eliminate confusion about who should hit the ball.

8. The partner with the stronger serve should serve first in every set. This will offer a better chance of getting off to a good start, and the first server will get to serve more often in a set than the partner. A possible exception to this rule is when the wind is a factor. The weaker server might have a better chance of holding serve with the wind, and the stronger server can probably win the serve with or without the benefit of the wind.

9. When the odds do not dictate hitting to a particular spot on the court, hit to the weaker player. If one partner is significantly weaker than the other, forget about percentages and play the majority of shots to that side of the court. If the stronger partner tries to cover for him or her, hit to the place left open.

MIXED DOUBLES

In social mixed doubles there are some unwritten rules to be considered. Those rules are mostly "Do Nots," such as (1) do not deliberately smash a setup directly at the weaker partner, (2) do not hit a disproportionate number of shots to the weaker partner, and (3) do not intimidate the weaker player on a team by hitting hard shots to him or her at the net. The idea is to have a good time, to let everyone get into the action, and to get out of the match in good physical and emotional health.

In tournament or match competition, however, these rules do not apply. Competitive mixed doubles should be played exactly like men's or women's doubles. Serves should be hit with the velocity and to the place in the service court most likely to produce a winning point, regardless of a player's sex. Shots should be directed to the weaker player on a team if the situation calls for that shot. Each player—man and woman—should cover his or her side of the court. The man should not cut in front of his partner unless percentage tennis would call for the same tactic in men's doubles. If the man poaches too often or hogs groundstrokes, he weakens his team's position by leaving part of the court open for the return. He also demeans his partner. He should pay the consequences for both acts. Given the levels of men's and women's tennis today, playing mixed doubles like men's or women's doubles probably means that the team with the stronger woman will win. This is especially true if the woman on the team can play well at the net. In the past, women have been hesitant about developing a net game, but that is changing now.

Positioning in mixed doubles should depend on which side of the court each partner can play best. There are some tennis strategists who claim that the crucial points are played on the odd court and that the stronger partner should line up on that side when the other team serves. Not only is the argument weak, but even if it were true, the advantage of having each player play from the side on which he or she is most effective and comfortable outweighs the crucial points theory. If the weaker partner is not an effective net player, that player should play from a baseline position when the stronger partner is receiving the serve. If the receiver's partner is a good volleyer and if the receiver can effectively return the serve, the receiver should begin the point from the baseline and the other player should start on the service line. On strong service returns, the receiver's partner should move in closer to the net and on weak returns he or she should retreat to the baseline. If both partners can play the net, they should both advance to a volleying position as soon as possible. Server and partner should begin points from about the same place they would in men's or women's doubles. If the server is weak, the player at the net might be positioned a bit closer to the center of the court in order to cover more ground on the return of serve. This tactic is not restricted to mixed doubles.

The partner with the stronger serve should begin serving for a team each set. There should be no racket spinning or polite questions about who wants to serve first. The man or woman who can do the best job should do it and do it first—no question about it.

Since mixed doubles usually has the least priority in practice and playing time, as compared to singles and men's or women's doubles, use as many shots as you can that create teamwork problems between partners. Moving the ball around the court as much as possible is a good way to manipulate the other team. Lobs are especially effective since one player has to give way to the other or the partners have to change positions on the court before hitting. Drop shots will also cause the other team to move out of their normal positions, thus creating open spots for subsequent shots.

Finally, make the mixed doubles team do what its members do not want to do. If either player is shy about playing the net, make that player come to the net by hitting short shots. If the team is very aggressive and always coming to the net, use the lob to keep the partners off balance. If one partner wants to dominate, make that player get out of position to do it. If the partners are not used to playing together, hit a lot of shots down the middle to create confusion about who will play the ball.

Take mixed doubles seriously. There are very few good teams, so the road to the top may be easier for you and your partner than in singles or doubles. Age and experience playing together are at least as important as youth and strength, so a good team can keep winning for a long time.

4

Playing Intelligently

CONCENTRATION

Concentration means the direction of attention to a single task or object. In tennis the task is to play the game as well as possible and the object is the tennis ball. There are many natural and man-made obstacles which can prevent you from concentrating on either the game or the ball. Before you get too involved in trying to attain a higher level of concentration, be sure that you want to. If you are one of the thousands of players who just want to go out, hit the ball, and have a good time, do not worry about directing all of your attention all of the time to the game you are playing. There is a great deal of enjoyment in talking with friends, socializing, being out of doors, watching others play, and just generally relaxing. However, if you are one of those players who is set on becoming highly skilled, competitive, and very serious about tennis, there are some problems and solutions when it comes to concentration.

The key to concentration is to block out as much as you can from your mind, leaving only the game to think about. Obviously that is almost impossible when you consider that tennis matches usually last from one to three hours. Nobody has an attention span that long. So the goal becomes one of mentally eliminating as many distractions as possible while you are on the court. First, consider some of the obstacles to concentration that are around the court where you are playing.

People are a major block to concentration. There are people on the courts next to you—talking, playing, hitting balls onto your court, and occasionally getting in your way or in your line of vision. Ignore them as much as you can without being discourteous. Do not watch their matches, even if their matches are more interesting than yours. Do not try to keep up with their scores. Play your own match. If your curiosity gets the best of you, get it out of your system by asking what the score is at a time when their match will not be interrupted. There may also be people in the stands or near your court watching your match. Keep your eyes out of the stands. Some players find it difficult to keep from glancing around to see who saw that last shot. If you are counting the house, you are not concentrating on what is happening on your court.

Even people on your own court can hinder your concentration. Some players may deliberately try to distract you or interrupt your thinking with an assortment of gamesmanship maneuvers. Some of the more popular methods of distraction are stalling instead of playing continuously, talking to you or to spectators, being overly dramatic after a point has been completed, and giving you a bad call just to upset you. There are two ways to handle these situations without totally losing your concentration. The first is to decide that nothing your opponent can do will bother you. If you expect trouble from an opponent or even if you get it unexpectedly, you must make a conscious decision that you will retain your poise and concentration regardless of what happens. That is a difficult enough task in itself and it becomes even more difficult if you are losing. Then, even minor irritations become magnified. It is a lot easier to concentrate when you are winning than when you are getting beat. If a non-aggressive policy does not work, then you might as well confront the person who is bothering you and try to solve the problem before the match continues. There is no use putting up with distractions if you are going to let worrying about them interfere with your game. If you are thinking about the problems, you are not thinking about tennis. Stop the match, call your opponent to the net, and state what is bothering you. If he or she refuses to cooperate, ask for an umpire or get a ruling from the tournament referee, if there is one. If the match is supposed to be merely a social one, do a better job of selecting opponents. It would be better to walk off the court than to become so incensed that an incident or loss of friendship might occur.

Once a match begins, try not to worry too much about how good your opponent is. Even if he or she is great, you are stuck with each other, and it is best to go ahead and play your kind of game. If you walk around on tiptoes or fear that every shot will be a winner, you will play below your capability. If you can relax a little and play each point rather than worrying about the outcome of the match, you may even play better than you usually do. Superior players frequently bring out the best in inferior opponents. On the other hand, do not let your mind wander if you are playing someone who you should easily beat. Be nice, but try just as hard on every point as you would against someone who is your equal on the court. If you can win 6-0, do it. Never throw points or games in a match because you feel sorry for the person on the other side of the net. If an opponent cannot challenge your tennis skills, make the match a challenge to your concentration. Save your compassion for social tennis.

Noise can be a distraction if you are not used to playing where the noise level is high. If people are making enough noise to warrant a legitimate complaint, either tolerate it or ask the people to be quieter. If the noise is coming from traffic, from work being done near the courts, or from passersby, learn to live with the noise or choose a quieter place to play. Actually, once you learn to play with a lot of noise, your concentration should improve. If you can concentrate when it is noisy, you can surely concentrate better in quiet surroundings. Players who learn to play on public courts probably have an advantage over club players in this respect.

Some players allow the weather, especially the wind, to interfere with concentration. The solution to this problem may be to make it a point to practice as much as possible when it is windy. If you can adapt your game to windy conditions instead of worrying about them, that will be one less obstacle to concentrating on your game.

In spite of all of these outside distractions, most of the problems of concentration come from within our own heads. We let our minds wander, we think about families, jobs, or studies, we worry about people seeing us make a bad shot, and we think about a thousand other things. Since it is impossible to cut out all non-tennis thoughts, you can at least try to eliminate the most obvious ones. First, play one point at a time. Try to remember that your opponent is not likely to hit any shot that you have not at least seen before this match. Have a plan on each point. Do not just wait to see what happens. You should know after a while where you want to place the ball, what your opponent does best, what he or she has trouble doing, and where you want to be on the court. If you are playing somebody better than you, you may not be able to carry out your plan, but at least start out with one, even if the plan is to keep the ball in play as long as possible.

Avoid unnecessary talking. Too many players conduct eulogies after every lost point. They moan, groan, curse, shout, reprimand themselves, coach themselves, and even appeal to the heavens for help. If you are talking about a point, you are probably talking about one that has already been completed and that you can do nothing about. Instead of dwelling on the last point, think about the next one. Where am I going to hit the serve? Where is my opponent going to serve? Am I fresh enough to get to the net? Should I take it easy on this point? Do I play conservatively or aggressively on the next shot?

Also avoid talking to your opponent. Do not be rude, but do not get carried away with compliments after good shots or chatting during side changes. If you really want to concentrate, 99 percent of your talking during a match should consist of giving the score and calling shots out when they hit beyond the line. Never call shots "good" or "in" during the point. Just hit the ball.

Do not give up after a bad shot. You are in the point until the ball goes into the net, goes out of bounds, or bounces twice. Some players stop thinking and trying when the opponent has a setup. Make your opponent put the ball away. Do not concede anything. Your opponent could blow an easy shot and you could retrieve a would-be winner. Tenacity is a good sign that you are concentrating, and it can be demoralizing to the other player. Do not give up after you have lost a point. Games, sets, and matches can take a long time to complete. Every player is going to lose points, miss setups, and occasionally be embarrassed by a good opponent. You have too many problems in front of you during a match to be worrying about how bad you looked on one or two shots. Your time for the super shot will come if you have the patience to wait for it. A few bad points are part of the game; do not let them get you down.

Your concentration should improve if you practice as seriously as you play matches. Try to follow the suggestions already discussed every time you walk onto the courts. If you can develop the ability to block out distractions during practice sessions, concentrating in matches should be easier because you will have fewer outside distractions, greater motivation to play well, and better rewards if you win. Characteristics such as steadiness, poise, tenacity, silence, and concentration can be learned just as strokes can be learned. We do not inherit tennis behavior; we *learn* to act and think the way we do on the court.

Now what *should* you think about during a match? Since people can only direct their attention to one thing at a time, a priority of thoughts has to be established. At the top of the list is the tennis ball. "Keep your eye on the ball" should be more than a frequently used platitude. If you are serving, watch the ball until it leaves your racket strings. If you are receiving the serve, focus on the ball while it is still in the tossing hand of the server. Follow it with your eyes from the toss to the point of contact, across the net, and into your racket. Do not worry about whether the serve is in or out until after you have swung at the ball. There is no penalty for calling a shot out after you hit it. Continue concentrating on the ball throughout the point. Watch it when you and your opponent are preparing to hit and when you are hitting.

The second item on the concentration priority list is your opponent. As the ball leaves your racket, you will have a second or two to watch where your opponent is on the court and how he or she is going to hit the next shot. The place to give special attention is the face of the other player's racket. If you watch anything else to the exclusion of the racket and the ball, you can be faked out of position. Immediately after the ball is hit for the return to you, you must at least be aware of where your opponent is going to position himself or herself on the court. In this situation, your mind will have to move rapidly back and forth between priority items. You have to be observant enough to know whether your opponent is going to come to the net, return to the center of the baseline, or move to one side of the backcourt. Within a split second your attention must again return to the ball.

The third priority item on your think list is the method of hitting the ball. You are much better off if you automatically move into the proper position rather than having to think about it. Since preparation for a stroke happens at the same time you are trying to concentrate on the ball, you cannot literally think about both things simultaneously. If your strokes are grooved to the point of thoughtless but effective preparation, you can devote full attention to the ball.

As if trying to direct attention to the ball, your opponent, and your own form were not enough, there are other factors worthy of your attention. The score in the game, the set score, the weather, your physical condition, your opponent's condition, and your game plan are all worth thinking about during a match. The time to do that thinking is between points and games, not while the ball is in play.

Become as totally absorbed in the match you are playing as possible. Try to isolate your playing from the rest of your life for the short period of time you are on the court. Forget for a while that there are many other things in your life more important than playing a game. If you can (and want to), create a temporary attitude in which the next point, game, or set is more important than family, friends, or society. It is doubtful that you can accomplish that, but if you set that standard as a goal, any progress toward that attitude should improve your game by improving your concentration.

ANTICIPATION

As you get better at the game, you may be faced with a frustrating problem. Your strokes probably look as good as those of others who have been playing as long as you have; you have begun to utilize a game plan of sorts rather than being forced into a style of play by your opponent; but you are frequently losing to players of seemingly equal ability because you do not know how to anticipate what is about to happen during a point. Your opponents know what you are going to do before you do it, and when you think you have the advantage in a particular situation, you lose the point because you have been "out-anticipated."

Much of what tennis players refer to as anticipation is simply knowing what to expect through years of experience. If a player learns the game before he is fifteen years old and continues to play regularly, by the time he reaches his thirties he has had twenty years of seeing shots and being in every conceivable court situation. With that kind of experience backlog, many older players can defeat younger ones even though the youngsters have the physical edge.

However, you can do three things to make up the anticipation gap between yourself and more experienced players: you can learn basic tennis strategy; you can familiarize yourself with your opponents' playing habits; and you can watch for tip-off signs.

If you know basic tennis strategy, you will know what most players should do in a given situation. In other words, what do the principles of sound tennis dictate in this situation? If you are playing someone who does not know anything about tennis strategy, you do not even have to worry about closing this part of the gap; it is already closed. But if your opponent knows what he should do, then you should know, also. An entire chapter in this book has been devoted to strategy, so you can test yourself on your tennis strategy I.Q. Here are some sample questions:

1. What is the primary target area for first serves?

2. Where should most baseline groundstrokes be directed?

3. Should approach shots be hit down the line, down the middle, or crosscourt? Why?

4. Where should volleys be hit?

5. To which side of your opponent should you hit lobs?

6. How often should you try to ace an opponent?

7. Should approach shots be hit for winners?

8. When should you let the ball bounce before hitting an overhead smash?

9. From which position on the court should you attempt drop shots?

10. Which of the two serves is more likely to be hit with topspin?

11. Where should you stand to serve in singles?

12. Where should you stand to serve in doubles?

13. Where should you stand when your partner is serving?

14. Where should you stand when your partner is receiving?

15. Which partner should hit shots that come down the middle of the court?

16. What kind of strategy would you use against a retriever? Against a big hitter?

17. How would you change your strategy if you were playing in windy conditions?

18. When should you poach in doubles?

19. When you poach, where should your volleys be directed?

20. When should you advance to the net in singles?

21. How would your strategy change if you were playing in extremely hot weather?

22. How would your strategy change if you were playing on a fast court?

23. How would your strategy change if you were playing on a slow court?

24. In doubles, where should you hit the ball if both opponents are at the net?

25. When should you choose to begin a match on a particular side rather than to serve first? Why?

The second thing you can do to close the anticipation gap is to find out what your opponents usually do in certain situations. All players fall into patterns of play, and if you can figure out what their habits are, you can make a relatively accurate guess about what is going to happen during a point. Look for favorite shots, favorite sides, combinations of shots used, strengths, weaknesses, and idiosyncrasies. If you are going to play a match against an unfamiliar opponent, talk to someone who has played that person. If you cannot do that, you are going to have to be especially observant during the first part of your match in order to learn what his or her pattern of play is. You may even consider making mental or written notes about your regular opponents.

Assuming that you know some basic tennis strategy, and after you have gathered all the information you can about an opponent, you are still faced with the most important immediate question: What is my opponent going to do on this shot? Here are some suggestions that will not replace twenty years of experience, but which may be enough to make the difference between winning a match and losing it. Remembering what has already been said about concentration, you cannot look for all of these tip-off signs at once. Just keep them in mind and use them when you get a chance.

1. *Watch your opponent's eyes prior to the serve.* Many players, even those in the advanced group, inadvertently look at the spot where they plan to serve just before they toss the ball. If you are watching your opponent's eyes closely enough, you can detect this tip-off sign and adjust accordingly. It may mean moving a step or two to the right or left, changing grips, or just having more confidence and purpose in your service return. Whatever it does for you, it may give you an advantage in games where your opponent is serving—games many players expect to lose.

2. *Watch your opponent's feet as he or she prepares to hit ground-strokes.* A closed stance (one in which the feet are more or less parallel to the alley or one in which the foot closer to the net crosses over in front of the back foot) usually indicates that the next shot is more likely to go down the line or straight ahead than anywhere else. An open stance (one in which the foot closer to the net does not come around to the parallel position) might be an indication that a crosscourt shot is coming.

3. *Watch your opponent's racket head as the backswing is taken.* If the racket head starts low and moves in a vertical motion rather than a motion horizontal to the court, watch for the topspin shot. When a shot is hit with topspin, the sound will be the same and the motion just as rapid, but the shot will have less velocity than a flat shot; it will rise fast, drop fast, and then take an unusually high bounce. If the racket head is drawn straight back, the return is likely to be flat, with good pace, and low to the net. If the racket head goes back high, watch for the chop (underspin). The chop will float a little, bounce lower than other shots, and slow down after the bounce.

4. *Watch the ball—even when it is on the other side of the net.* All tennis players learn that they should keep their eyes on the ball as they hit. Few have been taught to watch the ball as the other player prepares to hit. For example, when a righthander serving from the right side tosses the ball up toward the right side of the body, that player is likely to serve the ball closer to the middle of the court. If the server tosses the ball across the body toward the left, watch for the serve to go to the outside of the service court. Also watch how the ball bounces before your opponent hits a groundstroke. The ball may slide before it bounces, causing the player to hit up. It may hit a line, crack, or object on the court, throwing your opponent's timing off. The ball may bounce closer to your opponent than expected, causing him or her to rush the shot and usually causing the ball to be hit up and with backspin.

5. *Be aware of the court position of your opponent.* In certain situations a player can do only certain things. For example, you can usually

return a smash only with a lob, and a hard serve only with a block or chip. If you are running backward to retrieve a shot with your backhand, you probably cannot return the ball with power and it will probably go down the line. If you return a shot high to your backhand side, your return will probably go crosscourt. If you are stretching forward for a ball, you are more likely to hit up on it than if you were hitting from the side. If a shot comes directly at you, you are less likely to make a return shot with an angle than you would with a shot hit to either side of where you are. These are just a few examples of what most players can and cannot do with certain shots. If you know what your opponent can do from his or her position in relation to the shot you hit, you can move into the best position to make your next shot.

6. *Cover the open spot on the court.* If you cannot pick up any other tip-off sign in tennis, there is still a way you can anticipate what is likely to happen on many shots: always be conscious of where your side of the court is open. There is so much movement in tennis, there is a constantly changing pattern of places on the court which are alternately closing and opening. If you know that by moving to hit one shot you are, at the same time, leaving an open spot, you can expect the ball to be hit there. Do not wait to see if the ball is going to go in that direction. Assume that is where the ball will be hit and begin to move toward the open space. Here are some examples.

To return a serve in the deuce court, you have to move into the alley, leaving a big hole in the left side of the backcourt. As you make your return, you should immediately recover to close the space you created for your opponent.

Your opponent is at the net, you are in the right side of the backcourt. You hit a shot down the line. The most likely return will be a crosscourt volley, so as soon as you have hit your groundstroke, start moving to the other side of your baseline.

You rush the net behind a forcing shot. By moving close to the net, you have left a vacuum in your entire backcourt area. Be conscious of the possibility that your opponent will lob.

You are playing well behind your baseline and your opponent has established a position in the forecourt. If you return a shot down the middle, your opponent could easily hit a drop shot. Be ready to advance quickly in case that happens.

In doubles, anytime your partner has to go off of the court to retrieve a shot, you should drift toward his or her side of the court to cover the gap left by the movement. Your partner can let you know when he or she has recovered enough to play that side of the court without any help from you.

You are at the net and your partner serves. The return is a lob over your head. While your partner moves behind you to return the lob, you should drift across the court and back to a position approximately on the service line near the center of the court. At that spot you have closed the hole and you are in a position to return the next shot hit by your opponents.

Careful observation of these tip-off signs, combined with knowledge of tennis strategy and of your opponent's habits, will enable you to make a good guess about what is going to happen in many situations. Anticipation requires as much or more concentration as hitting the ball. Making decisions based on partial evidence is better than having no evidence at all, and by anticipating a shot, a player can move into position sooner and get his racket ready. True, we are talking about only seconds and fractions of seconds in terms of preparing for the next shot, but even that little amount of time is precious and will become more precious as you improve and play against better players.[1]

USING PSYCHOLOGICAL ADVANTAGES

Remember that the better player usually wins a tennis match. So although there are things you can do to improve the physical and mental aspects of your game, there is no one psychological tactic that is going to enable you to knock off that person who always beats you. Also remember that it is difficult to psych out people with whom you play frequently. After a while you get to know each other so well that nothing anybody does is a surprise. However, in matches or tournaments when you compete against players who are about your speed, you may be able to use some psychological moves to your advantage. It should be emphasized that you should not spend so much time or effort trying to psych out somebody that you neglect the two most important aspects of winning tennis: good shots and sound strategy. Within this context, here are some suggestions that may give you a psychological edge in certain situations.

Before a match begins, do not offer any information about your game or your ability that may hurt your chances when play begins. Weekend tennis players are almost neurotic when it comes to worrying that an

[1] Brian Chamberlain and Jim Brown, "Anticipation and the Intermediate Tennis Player," *Athletic Journal*, 51, no. 9 (May 1972), 38.

unknown opponent may be a great tennis player. There are all sorts of little pre-match games played off the courts in which players try to find out how good the other person is. Questions are asked such as, "Are you ranked?" "Is she seeded?" "How did you do against Fred?" "Did you ever play college tennis?" "Has she ever played Arlene?" "How does he play on this kind of surface?" If a prospective opponent finds out that he or she frequently beats someone who has beaten you, that player's confidence may zoom. Do not volunteer that kind of information. On the other hand, if your opponent is nosy about how good you are and if you have something to say about your game that might be intimidating, do it. Do not force anything, just subtly and casually let it be known by your responses to the questions. The less your opponent knows about you, the better off you are. Reveal your game, style, and ability during the match, not before it.

Once you get onto the court for the warmup period, warm up seriously. Do not waste time chattering. Play shots on the first bounce as much as you can without wearing yourself out. Establish an attitude of serious tennis. Make sure that you get to practice all the shots that you expect to use when the match begins. When you practice serving, loosen up adequately, but do not necessarily hit your best serves. If you can save your match serves for the first game, you may pick up a few points on un-returned serves just because it takes a while for your opponent to get used to your style, velocity, or spin. If you use your good serves during the warmup, your opponent gets a chance to practice returning them. At the same time you are not showing your best serves, you should practice re-turning balls he or she serves during the warmup. You will get used to the other player's kind of serve, and you may also demonstrate that you can handle anything that player has for you.

Once the match starts, move in a step or two on your opponent's second serve, and do it at a time when he or she can see you moving in. The first reason for this move is that the second serve is likely to be hit with less velocity than the first and probably be hit shorter in the service court. By moving forward, you will be in a better position to make the return. If you stay back, you will have to run up and get into position before you hit. The psychological reason for advancing at a time when your opponent can see you is that the move can intimidate the server. By stepping toward the other player as he or she serves, you are sending a nonverbal message which says: "Your second serve is weak enough for me to move up on you; I am going to do something special with my return; and I am taking charge of this point." One other comment about returning the second serve: occasionally run around the weak second serve hit to your backhand side and really tee off with a blistering fore-hand shot. Even if it does not win that point, it will give your opponent something to think about the next time he or she gets ready to hit that serve.

During a match, mix up your shots. Do not fall into a pattern of play that your opponent can predict and anticipate. If you are a power player, occasionally use some junk shots just to keep your opponent off balance. If you are a retriever, show that you are capable of hitting the strong passing shot. Mixing up shots may even mean hitting a low-percentage shot occasionally. Be judicious about when to attempt high-risk shots, but the person you are playing should always have to think, "What is that guy going to do next?" It would be even better if your opponent thinks he or she knows exactly what you are going to do, only to see you do something completely different. The more things the other player has to worry about, the better off you are. Do not force shots to prove you are unpredictable, just use the unpredictable shot occasionally—preferably when losing a point will not cost you a game or a set.

One of the best potential psychological weapons at your disposal is your temperament. One good weekend player tells this story: "I had a match against a guy who was good enough to beat me as often and as badly as he wanted to. He was ranked in the state, experienced, had all the shots, and was in good shape. When the match started, I played as well as I have ever played in my life. I hit shots consistently that I had never been able to control before. At the same time, my opponent was playing terribly. He was missing easy shots, double faulting, making mental errors, and generally playing poor tennis. Yet, even with the score 5-1 in my favor in the first set, he never said a word, never looked worried about losing, complimented my good shots, and did not blink an eye after his bad shots. You would have thought he was the player ahead, 5-1. His attitude got to me. Here I was playing tennis as well as I could ever hope to play; here he was looking like a hacker; and he did not appear the least bit distressed about his chances of coming back and winning. He won, 7-6, 6-1. Judging only by his court presence, the score could have been 6-0, 6-0."

The moral of that story is to maintain your poise regardless of what the score is. If you get behind and begin to talk to yourself, curse, make excuses, complain about bad luck, and act like you are beaten, your attitude has to give your opponent a psychological lift. Do not give that advantage. Try to present a calm, confident, determined front no matter how bad things are going. If you come back and win, you will have proven to yourself that you can do it, and you will let the other player know that regardless of the score, you are always in the match. Your opponent will never be completely confident of beating you until the match is over.

There are several things you can do in doubles to make the other team worry about things they should not have to worry about. One thing you can do is poach. Let the other team know that you are a threat to go at any time your partner is serving. Be sure not to risk the loss of a crucial point by poaching just to prove you can do it, but be selective and get out there to pick off a service return now and then. Even if you lose that point, you have given the opponents one other little problem to think about. If you find out that one of the players on the other team really has problems with the return of serve, poach frequently. Intimidate the player as much as you can. Also, fake the poach at times; once you have established the fact that you are a threat at the net, take a quick step toward the middle just before the service return, but get back to protect your side of the court. Do not jump around at the net; make your fake look as much like an actual poach as possible. Let your partner know that you may try a fake poach, so he or she will not pull up and be faked by your move instead of the opponent.

If you play doubles regularly with the same partner, consider using signals when your team is serving. For example, the partner at the net can show a closed fist behind the back to indicate he or she will not poach, one finger to show an intention to poach on the first serve, and two fingers to mean poaching on both serves. Signals also give the other team something to think about, and they can also help the serving team because the server will know exactly what part of the court must be covered after the serve. Signals work best when both players are used to watching for and responding to the signs. If a team is not accustomed to using signals, they can do more harm than good.

When you are returning the serve in doubles, there are at least two tactics you can use. First, glance at the alley being protected by the net player just before the serve. Just as a baseball pitcher looks a runner back to the bag, look your opponent back toward his alley. Make sure that player sees your glance. If your look keeps the person a little more honest about protecting his or her side of the court and not getting a good jump to poach, you will have more room to hit the crosscourt return. Second, hit down the line every once in a while and try to lob over the net player's head on some service returns. If you try either shot early in the match, you may force your opponent to play more conservatively than if there were no threat of shots directed to his or her side of the court. Regardless of when you hit down the line or try the lob, these shots keep you from falling into a predictable pattern of service returns. While percentage tennis says that the return should go crosscourt or down the middle, those shots will be easier to execute if your opponents think you might not always hit the percentage shot.

Finally, keep your eyes and ears open for conversations between your doubles opponents. Do not turn your back to them. You will be surprised to find out how much you can learn about what is going to happen if you watch and listen to what is being said. Players at the net will sometimes tell their partners (without a signal) that they are going to poach. Servers might tell their partners that they are going to serve to the forehand or backhand. They might mention a weakness they have spotted. If you are not paying attention to what is being said or indicated, you might miss a tip that could win a point or game for your team.

PERSONALIZING YOUR GAME

As you play more and more tennis, your game will begin to take shape. You will be known as a certain kind or style of player. Your strengths and weaknesses will become more obvious to you and to your opponents. Your strategic approach to tennis will also become somewhat predictable. Even though your game will be determined to a degree by factors over which you have no control, there are some things you can do to shape your own game. You can become the kind of player you want to be within the limits of your ability, experience, opposition, amount of time to practice, and competitive attitude. Players who do not believe this or who do not have the interest or time to mold their own games are destined to go out and play without a style of their own, erratically, and with very little control over what happens on the court.

Those of you who think you do have some control over your tennis destiny should first look very closely at the things you do best on the court. Most players have one or two shots which they can really execute well. For some it is the big serve, for others a powerful forehand, a consistent backhand, or a good net game. Whatever it is you do best, try to create situations during your matches so that you get to use your best shots. If consistency is your strength, forget about trying to make spectacular shots and make the other player beat himself. If you have a strong forehand, play a little to your backhand side so that more shots have to be hit to your forehand. If you are comfortable playing at the net, get up there as often as you can. If your backhand is good, play a bit toward the forehand side of the court.

At the same time you cash in on your good shots, you can do two things about your weak shots. You can avoid having to hit them during a match. In the same way that you run around certain shots in order to hit your strongest strokes, you can move on the court in such a way as to avoid hitting weaker strokes. If you are weak at the net, there is no rule that says you have to move up there to play the game. If you are inconsistent, you can hit forceful shots to end points quickly rather than letting your opponent wait for your mistakes. The second thing you can do about weak strokes is to use matches to work on improving problem areas. Play against people you know will try to exploit your weaknesses. Sometimes if your opponent hits enough shots to one weak stroke you have, that stroke begins to get stronger because of the practice you are getting.

In order to learn exactly what your strengths and weaknesses are, you may consider charting your matches. In some cases, what you perceive to be happening during a match and what is actually happening are not the same. In the heat of a match, a few good shots or bad shots may stand out in your mind even though more subtle facets of your game were the determining factors in winning and losing. If you can get someone to watch a couple of your matches, it is relatively simple to keep a record of how points and games are won and lost. Charting merely involves recording how a series of points were completed. There are elaborate systems used by college coaches and observers of professional tennis players, but the average weekend beginner or intermediate could use something like this:

GAME SCORE	POINT	SERVER – GARVIN	SET SCORE
0 -15	double fault		
15-15	serve return error		
30-15	forehand passing shot		1–0 (Garvin)
30-30	overhead smash error		
40-30	first-serve ace		
game	backhand error		

GAME SCORE	POINT	SERVER – STONE	SET SCORE
15- 0	backhand volley error (bhv-x)		
15-15	double fault (df)		
15-30	backhand error (bh-x)		
15-40	forehand passing shot (fh-p)		0–2 (Garvin)
30-40	first-serve ace (A-1)		
game	lob winner (L)		

GAME SCORE	POINT	SERVER – GARVIN	SET SCORE
15- 0	fh-x		
15-15	fhv		
30-15	fhv-x		
30-30	bh-p		
30-40	fh-x		2–1 (Garvin)
40-40	A-2		
ad in	bh-x		
deuce	df		
ad out	fh-x		
game	fhv-x		

It is obvious that several games will have to be charted in order for a pattern to be established, but if someone has the time to watch you and to make notes, it could help you to find out without a doubt what the strong and weak points of your game are. The possibilities for abbreviating or coding your shots are unlimited. There is also much that could be added to the information shown here. If you decide to keep a chart on your matches, begin with a simple system and add to it if the results warrant a more thorough record of how you are playing.

Once you know what you can and cannot do, develop a style of play with which you are comfortable. If you know what kind of player you are, you can set realistic goals and develop a style that you like. If you are always seeking something new or different with your game, you can never have the security of knowing who you are on the court. You will tend to second guess your shots and your strategy. This does not mean that you should stop trying to improve your game; just spend more time in developing what you already have than in trying to revamp your style of play. Do not worry about the books which teach only one way to play tennis. There is nothing wrong with pushing if pushing wins. A two-handed backhand may not be right for 99 percent of the players, but it may be best for you. Running around your backhand is not recommended by teaching professionals (and it should not be taught), but it may win points for you in some situations. Do what is best for *you*, as long as you are successful. If peculiarities in style begin to get you into trouble or prohibit you from developing your overall game, then consider making changes.

Play a game consistent with your physical capabilities. If you are middle-aged and get to exercise only a couple of times a week, be careful about playing the kind of tennis that overtaxes you. Either slow down your pace or play more doubles. Most people, as they get older, have to pace their game downward to compensate for the lack of time they can give to tennis. Toning the game down does not necessarily mean becoming less of a player. It just means that you have to rely more on technique, strategy, and consistency than on physical strength and speed. The situation is comparable to that of the baseball pitcher who begins his career as a fastballer and who develops into a finesse pitcher once the fast ball leaves him. He still gets good results; he simply changes the means of getting those results.

Play a game consistent with the amount of time you have to practice. Tennis is a difficult sport in which to maintain skill levels. If you cannot play several times a week, forget about trying to play a game that requires you consistently to make extremely difficult shots such as hard serves, forcing volleys, and strong overhead smashes. You cannot play shots close to the lines as a normal part of your game unless you practice those shots frequently. Drop shots and lobs require a delicate touch that is not easy to maintain without regular play. That leaves the weekend player with challenging, but limited groundstrokes, volleys, and well-placed serves in his repertoire.

Play against people who can challenge your skills. If you play only against people you can easily defeat, you will probably win without having to think about and execute demanding shots. You will get the satisfaction of winning a match, but it is doubtful that you will benefit from playing. If you play people of your caliber, you can practice your good shots and improve on your weak ones at the same time. If you play against someone who is out of your class, consider it a free lesson and learn as much as you can while you are being drubbed.

As much as possible, force your opponents to play your style of game. If you do not have a game, you are going to have to change your style of play every time you walk onto the court. If you know what your game plan is, you can at least begin the match by sticking to your shots. If you try to blast with the big hitter or push against the retriever, you will never develop the consistency to play your own game. If your opponent is a lot better than you are, you will not be able to control the match. However, against lesser players, you will be more successful if you play it your way, not theirs.

Finally, be honest with yourself about your commitment to the game. If you are not interested in playing serious tennis, try not to get upset about the quality of your playing. Occasional players and recreational players do not have the right to expect their shots and games to go well. The players who get out there several times a week and work hard to develop their strokes have the luxury of being frustrated when things go badly. Tennis is not an easy game to play well. Everyone who plays deserves to have a good time. Only those who put a lot into tennis deserve to have a good time and to play consistently winning tennis.

5

Improving
Without Playing

IMPROVING BY READING

One of the by-products of the tennis boom has been a huge increase in the number of books, articles, tapes, brochures, films, and other audio-visual aids related to tennis instruction. While some of the new reading material is good, a lot of it is not. Since the player who is new to the game may also be new to the literature, here are some ideas that may help you in deciding what to read.

First, select tennis articles and books written for you as a player. There is material written for teachers, coaches, physical education instructors, fans, and others. Several books on the market try to reach more than one reading audience. For example, some books are written for players and teachers. If you are considering such a book, remember that 50 percent of its information is written for somebody else. If you are a player interested in improving your skills but not very interested in methods of teaching, coaching tennis teams, or organizing competition, buy a book or read an article for players only.

Second, try to find material that is written for players of your ability. There are books and articles written for beginners, intermediates, and advanced players. There is such a wide gap between the levels of play, it does little good for the player at one level to read about what should be done at a much higher or lower level. There is a classic book which deals with singles strategy, placement of shots, and percentage tennis. While the book is great for the advanced player, it is of little value to a person who is just beginning to play and whose primary concern is keeping the ball in play. There are several well-written books for beginners which contain information that has already been learned by most advanced players. Read the preface and the table of contents before buying a book. The information in those two sections should let you know for whom the book is written. A book's index might also give you an idea of its content. Incidentally, this book is written primarily for beginners and inter-mediates.

Consider the authors of the books or articles you choose to read. Do not assume that because the author is a famous player, he is also a good teacher, or that because he is a well-known teacher that he can write. Al-though there are some great players and teachers who can write clearly about how to play the game, most world class tennis personalities do not have the time, ability, or interest to sit down and write a book. Some of the great names in tennis teaching and writing are not names that the average sports page reader or tennis player would recognize (for example, Van der Meer, Van Horn, Barnaby, Murphy, Leighton). Before you spend too much time or money on the book or article, attempt to find out something about the author by reading the jacket cover or asking knowl-edgeable tennis people if they are familiar with a particular author's work.

At the risk of discouraging the sale of this book, it may be a good idea to spend more time reading articles and less time reading books. Articles usually read more easily, they are shorter, and they concentrate on fewer ideas than books. You can also get several instructional articles in one tennis magazine for a dollar or less, whereas books cost more money. You will also find that many authors who write books also write magazine articles which are taken from the books. In an article you may be getting the meat instead of the padding included in a whole book.

Whether you read a book or an article, try to pull out a few key ideas that will help your game. Trying to read a whole book or a long article and then incorporating all of that information into your game is impossible. That is like taking a five-hour tennis lesson; there is just too much for a person to comprehend and utilize. Select a chapter or two at a time to read, and then go out to try what you have learned. After you have made some progress on that phase of your game, go back and read another section or two.

Establish some kind of reading pattern for yourself. Concentrate on one phase of the game at a time. If you take a lesson, the pro does not try to cover strokes, strategy, psychological aspects, and conditioning in one session. Neither should you bounce from item to item without some kind of planned reading program. If you decided to really learn as much as you could about the serve by reading, and if you could read ten separate articles, think of what an expert you would become. After all, there is just so much information about a tennis stroke that can be put on paper. Set aside a time for your tennis reading. If you read only when you have nothing else to do, you probably will not read at all.

Finally, reread parts of books and articles. As with old movies and old letters, you will see something new or different every time you go back and look at them again. You cannot remember everything that is said during a tennis lesson, and that is probably just as well. Books and articles are written more concisely than normal conversation, but there are still so many facts per page, that some forgetting is inevitable. Reading those facts two or three times may reinforce the learning process.

Tennis Magazines

Magazines containing tennis-related material are usually directed toward one of three groups: tennis players and fans, tennis teachers and coaches, and persons with commercial tennis interests. Publications in the first group have news stories, tournaments results, features, editorial comments, columns, schedules of tennis events, instructional articles, and advertisements for tennis products and services. Here are the names and addresses of some of the more widely circulated magazines for players and fans:

British Lawn Tennis
"Lowlands," Wenhaston, Halesworth,
Suffolk 1P19 9DY, England

Racquets Canada
643 Yonge Street
Toronto 5, Ontario, Canada

Tennis
1255 Portland Place
Boulder, Colorado 80302

Tennis Illustrated
630 Shatto Place
Los Angeles, California 90005

Tennis U.S.A.
P.O. Box 2090
Radnor, Pennsylvania 19089

Tennis World
Royal London House, 171B High Street
Beckenham, Kent, BR3 1BY, England

World Tennis
15 Love Street
Marion, Ohio 43302

Tennis Books

Here is a list of books and authors which might be of interest to beginning and intermediate tennis players:

All About Tennis
Book of Tennis, Lumiere
Check List for Better Tennis, Bockus
The Code, Powell
Complete Beginner's Guide to Tennis, Lardner
Courtside Companion, Zweig
Extraordinary Tennis for the Ordinary Player, Ramo
Fireside Book of Tennis, Danzig and Schwed
Getting Started in Tennis, Meltzer
How to Beat Better Tennis Players, Fiske
How to Play Better Tennis, Tilden
Improving Your Tennis, Jones
Inner Game of Tennis, Gallwey
Inside Tennis, Leighton
Lobbing Into the Sun, Hopman
Match Play and Spin of the Ball, Tilden
Match Winning Tennis, Jones
Mixed Doubles, Graebner
Net Results: The Complete Tennis Handbook
Percentage Tennis, Lowe
Rod Laver's Tennis Digest, Laver
Sinister Tennis, Schwed
So You're Going to Take Tennis Seriously, Roberts
Speed, Strength, and Stamina: Conditioning for Tennis, Haynes
Sports Illustrated—Tennis, Talbert
Stroke Production in Tennis, Talbert and Olds
Tennis, Athletic Institute
Tennis, Faulkner and Weymuller
Tennis, Mason

Tennis, Pearce and Pearce

Tennis, Pelton

Tennis, Anyone?, Gould

Tennis Clinic, Van der Meer and Olderman

Tennis Everyone, Schultz

Tennis for Anyone, Palfrey

Tennis for Beginners, Murray

Tennis for Everyone, Addie

Tennis for Teenagers, Addie

Tennis for the Bloody Fun of It, Laver, Emerson, Tarshis

Tennis for Women, Gunter

Tennis: Learn to Volley First, Summerfield

Tennis Made Easy, Brecheen

Tennis Self Instructor, Driver

Tennis: The Hacker's Handbook, Pollack and Long

Tennis to Win, King

Tennis Weaknesses and Remedies, Meltzer

Tennis Without Mistakes, Eldred

Tennis Workbook, Kraft

Use Your Head in Tennis, Hartman

Weekend Tennis, Talbert

IMPROVING BY WATCHING

Most people watch tennis matches because the sport can be entertaining for spectators. But you can also watch to improve your game and to scout future opponents. If you want to improve by watching or if you want to get information that may help you beat somebody, there are ways to get more out of your observations.

With all of the tennis being played today, there are many places to watch good players. Professional tournaments, television, college matches, and local or regional tournaments all provide settings to improve your tennis by watching someone else play. Of these four places to watch, professional tournaments are probably the least beneficial for the observer who wants to learn. For one thing, the players are so skilled and so gifted athletically, that they cannot be compared to the average beginning or intermediate player. Many of the professionals have peculiarities in their styles of play that would not be appropriate for lesser players. Another reason why the professional tournaments are not the best places to observe for the sake of learning is that there are too many distractions. A person who goes to one of these events pays a lot of money to be entertained. There are celebrities to see, friends to talk with, scores to keep, things to buy, and many other sideshows to keep a person from religiously watching the mechanics of stroke production or court strategy. It is not impossible to learn by watching the pros; it is just very difficult.

Television is not a great place to learn much about tennis, either. While there are fewer distractions for the viewer, the nature of television makes observation of many aspects of the game almost impossible. On a small screen, the viewer does not get an accurate perspective on things like the velocity of the ball, trajectory, spin, or size and speed of the players. Everything seems to be miniaturized so much that the subtle aspects of the game are lost to the viewer. The observer can become involved in who is winning and losing, but not be aware of the finer points which might be helpful.

Perhaps the best two places to learn by watching are at matches between good college teams and at tournaments in your area which attract outstanding amateur players. The quality of play is good enough to learn something, the players are closer to the spectators in terms of physical capabilities, there are fewer distractions, and you can get close enough to the action to really watch what is happening. If you are interested enough to observe matches and have enough time to do so, watch the papers for announcements of tournaments and matches to be played in your area.

Once you decide to try to learn by watching, what should you watch for? First, look for the way strokes are produced by the players. Start with the preparation for shots. Most spectators cannot resist the temptation to watch the ball first and everything else if they get a chance. Watch what good players do after they hit a shot. How do they get ready for the next shot? Where do they move on the court? What parts of the court do they protect or leave unprotected? How do they move their feet in preparing for the next shot? How many steps do they take to get from the baseline to a volleying position? How long does it take them to get to that position? When and where do they plant their feet prior to a shot? In which direction do they turn the upper part of their body? Do they move toward the ball in a direct line or do they move in an indirect path? Where is the racket head while they are moving to hit a shot?

After spending some time concentrating on preparation, then try to answer these questions about the various strokes you are watching. Where is the racket head in relation to the waist of the hitters when contact is made? Is it below, above, or even with the belt? Where do the players make contact with the ball? Is it in front of, even with, or behind the body? Are shots hit with backspin, topspin, sidespin, or no spin? Do the players swing from the shoulder or the elbow? Do they use the wrist on some shots? Which shots? How do they transfer their weight as they hit? How high over the net do their groundstrokes travel? On the serve, how high do they toss the ball? At what point is contact made? What kind of spin is put on the serve? Is there a difference between first and second serves? What is the difference? How close to the net do the players stand on volleys? How much of a backswing do they take? Do they crouch to hit some shots? Where do they make contact with the ball on volleys? Do they use a full swing or restricted swing on smashes?

When you are tired of looking for little things in the strokes, think about match strategy for a while. Are shots being placed to particular spots on the court? Does the player who is winning use different strategy than the one who is losing? Does each player have a game plan? What are the game plans? If you were the player losing the match, what would you do differently? Are the players using percentage shots or do they gamble with high-risk shots?

The ultimate test of how well you have observed a match is to be able to answer many of the above questions about a specific player after the match has been played. Do you just know who won and remember a few good shots, or can you tell someone else exactly how a player executed the shots and used a strategic plan of attack? Even if you can remember the details of some players' style and approach to the game, it will not do you any good unless you can incorporate some of their strengths into parts of your game that are weak. As in reading about tennis, do not try to take in so much of someone else's game that you become confused. Find the player who can do something well that you cannot do effectively or consistently, and copy the way he or she does it. You must be able to imitate the movement of others to play tennis well. People are not born with an innate knowledge of how to hit a tennis ball correctly. They watch others, listen to what others say, read what others write, and then emulate styles of play within their own limits of movement. The good athlete can watch someone execute a series of physical movements and come very close to imitating those movements. The lesser athlete must work to make his body do what some people can do almost naturally. So when you observe that stroke that looks right to you, capture the total picture in your mind, then transfer the picture from your mind to your body.

If you watch a tennis match in order to scout a future opponent, you should be looking for other things. Your objective now is to learn how to beat this player. You will have a better chance of winning if you can answer some of the questions below about the player's game and then do something in your match to take advantage of the information you have gathered.

1. Who is the player?

2. Who did he (or she) play?

3. Who won?

4. What was the score?

5. What kind of surface was the match played on?

6. Did the surface affect his style of play? How?

7. Is he righthanded or lefthanded?

8. Generally, how would you describe his forehand, backhand, serve, forehand volley, backhand volley, and overhead smash?

9. Where does he usually place the first serve?

10. Where does he usually place the second serve?

11. Where should you stand to receive the serves?

12. What is his best shot?

13. What can you do to keep him from hitting his strongest shot?

14. What is his weakest shot?

15. What can you do to make him hit his weakest shot?

16. Does he have any unusual shot?

17. Does he prefer to play in the backcourt or at the net?

18. On which shots does he come to the net?

19. What percentage of overhead smashes does he hit in the court?

20. Can his smashes be retrieved?

21. Does he have a good lob?

22. Is he in good physical condition?

23. Can he keep the ball in play for long rallies?

24. Is he honest on line calls?

25. Assuming that you have a chance to beat this person, what are the two things you will have to do to win the match?

If you have all of that information about an opponent, you will be better prepared to play the match than 99 percent of all the tennis players in the world. Most people do not have the time to get that kind of report on a player before a match. If you do not have the time, consider writing down what you learn about an opponent after you have played together. You may play each other again. Remember that no matter how much you know about another player and no matter how well planned your strategy is, you have to be able to consistently keep the ball in play for your strategy to work. Until you reach a level where you can do that, you are not ready for scouting other players.

IMPROVING YOUR PHYSICAL CONDITION

While most people are vaguely aware that it would be good for them to be "in good shape," very few people really know what good physical condition means. The person who maintains proper muscle tone, an efficient cardiovascular system, and healthy lungs, and who eats a well-balanced selection of food, experiences a feeling of well-being that is unfamiliar to most people. Once you discover or rediscover how great this feeling can be, you are likely to stay at a high level of fitness.

If you play tennis several times a week, you are getting exercise, but whether or not you can attain total physical fitness depends not only on how often you play, but how strenuously you play and what you do physically besides playing tennis. Playing hard only once or twice a week may do more harm than not playing tennis at all. The idea is to play strenuously and regularly. If you are playing hard enough to raise your pulse rate to 140 beats a minute and to keep it there for periods of time consistent with your present capacity for work, consider that strenuous exercise. If you are not playing at that level, you may be having a good time, but you are doing very little to maintain or increase your respiratory and cardiovascular fitness.

There is no question that you can improve your tennis game by becoming more physically fit. You may have only enough time or interest to get your exercise on the courts. But if you want to reach a higher level of fitness and at the same time enhance your tennis without even going to the courts, there are ways to do it.

Running

Although jogging can be beneficial to the cardiovascular and respiratory systems of the body, it may not be the best kind of running for tennis players. Sprinting short distances—10 to 50 yards—seems to be more appropriate for tennis players than long-distance running. Several series of sprints three or four times a week can improve the cardiovascular system and simultaneously build strength in the muscles of the legs. Since tennis requires the player to run short distances, change directions, stop and start quickly, and make other quick movements, a running program which includes many repetitions of short distances can be very helpful. Jogging long distances can be advantageous, too, but not in ways that will specifically help the tennis player. Before you decide to do any kind of running to get into shape, consult a physician, a physical therapist, a physical educator, or someone else who knows you and what you are capable of doing physically. It is very dangerous to embark on a running program that is not consistent with your age, physical condition, and general health.

Isometric Exercises

Isometric exercises are those in which all of the fibers in a set of muscles fully contract, but do not move in doing so. They usually involve trying to pull, push, lift, or in some way move an immovable object. There are advantages and disadvantages of building strength and muscular fitness through isometrics. The advantages are: (1) they do not require as much time as traditional types of exercise do; (2) they require very little space; (3) not much equipment is needed; (4) they can be adapted for any set of muscles in the body; and (5) they do not make one look muscular. The disadvantages are: (1) they do not build endurance as well as do other forms of exercise; (2) they do not build strength at a full range of motion as some other strength programs do; and (3) they do not build bulk.

Isometrics for tennis players would be especially effective for building strength in the fingers, wrists, forearms, upper arms, and shoulders. You can perform isometric exercises for these areas of the body by swinging through any of your strokes—forehand, backhand, serve, forehand volley, backhand volley, or overhead smash—and holding your movement at the probable point of contact with the ball. You do not have to actually swing through to that point; you can just start the exercise by putting your racket and arm in the hitting position. At that point, restrict any further motion of the racket or arm by using a wall, fence, another person's hand, or anything else that will provide an immovable object. Exert as much force as you can against the immovable object for eight seconds, then rest and repeat the exercise. Rest and repeat it once more. Three eight-second maximum contractions a day for each of the strokes would be a good start for a strength-building program. Although the exercises described here involve muscles from the shoulders to the fingers, you can increase your strength in any part of your body through isometrics. Design your own exercises for whatever muscles need strengthening.

Isotonic Exercises

Isotonic exercise is muscle contraction with movement. Any movement, with or without weights, that overloads muscles and involves movement through a range of motion is an isotonic exercise. The advantages of isotonics are: (1) they increase the variety of methods you can use to become stronger; (2) they improve respiratory and cardiovascular fitness as well as physical strength; (3) strength is built through a range of motion instead of just at one point; and (4) your muscles will increase in size (if you consider that an advantage). The disadvantages of isotonic exercises are: (1) they are time consuming; (2) specialized equipment may be needed; (3) you may need a lot of space in which to exercise; and (4) it could make your muscles bigger, which may not be desirable for some people.

There are hundreds of ways to exercise isotonically. Here are a few of the ways which could help tennis players.

For fingers and wrists, attach a two- to five-pound weight to a length of cord and attach the cord to a handle the size of a broomstick; roll the weight up on the handle, first with the palms up, then with the palms down. Repeat the exercise as many times as you can without putting undue strain on the muscles being worked.

For arms and shoulders, do push-ups or modified push-ups; start with a few repetitions and increase the number by one each day. Get a five-pound dumbbell and do five to ten curls with each arm (a curl is done by holding the weight down at your side with your arm fully extended, then flexing the arm from the elbow, bringing the weight upward in front of your body). Swing a racket with a weighted racket cover on the racket head; begin with ten swings each for the serve, forehand, and backhand, and increase the number of repetitions by one each day you exercise. Swing a frying pan through twenty forehands and backhands every day. Squeeze a tennis ball 25 times the first day and increase by five each day thereafter. Swing two rackets at the same time in the same hand; do as many repetitions as you can without straining the arm muscles, then gradually increase the number of swings.

For the legs, run in place for one minute or whatever length of time is appropriate for you. Jump rope for the length of time your advisor says is good for you. Increase the strength in the leg muscles by doing toe lifts: a toe lift is performed by standing next to a wall or fence, holding on to the wall with one hand to keep your balance, and then extending your ankle joint by lifting your weight up on the toes of one foot; begin with ten or fifteen lifts daily on each foot. Find a bench or step that is securely fixed at a height of two or three feet; stand in front of the bench and step up on it with both feet, return to the floor or ground with both feet (one at a time), then repeat the up and down stepping for a period of time. Do not do this last exercise for a period longer than thirty seconds on the first day, unless you know you are physically fit enough to do it safely; you may increase the length of time as you get stronger.

A Packaged Exercise Program

If you are looking for a preplanned program of exercise to improve your fitness, here is one that can be done at home. The exercises in this program are designed for people who have already reached a reasonable level of fitness. The program should be modified to fit your needs and should be a supplement to your regular routine of playing tennis frequently.

MONDAY-WEDNESDAY-FRIDAY

5 minutes	Isometrics at point of contact on forehand, backhand, and serve; three 8-second repetitions
1 minute	Run in place
1 minute	Rest
1 minute	Run in place
1 minute	Rest
1 minute	Run in place
1 minute	Rest
5 minutes	Isometric leg lifts (sit down and put one ankle on top of the other; lift with one leg and hold it down with the other); three 8-second repetitions for each leg; rest one minute after every two repetitions
2 minutes	Squeeze a tennis ball with your racket hand; do as many repetitions as you can in 30 seconds, rest 30 seconds, repeat, and rest another 30 seconds

TUESDAY-THURSDAY-SATURDAY

1 minute	Run in place
1 minute	Rest
1 minute	Run in place
1 minute	Rest
1 minute	Run in place
1 minute	Rest
1 minute	Push-ups
1 minute	Swing weighted racket through the forehand
1 minute	Rest
1 minute	Swing weighted racket through the backhand
1 minute	Rest
1 minute	Swing weighted racket through the serve
2 minutes	Toe lifts; one minute for each leg
3 minutes	Wrist rolls; one minute with palms up; rest one minute; one minute with palms down

Establishing Guidelines

There is no one best program of physical conditioning. Every person should have a program that fits his or her special needs. In order to make your program effective, you should consider these guidelines:

1. Try to design a program that is enjoyable. If you dread doing the exercises, you will not continue with them. Setting goals, doing the exercises with a partner or with friends, and rewarding yourself might make things more interesting.

2. Start with modest goals of increasing strength. There is plenty of time to improve.

3. Overload the muscles being exercised, but without risking injury. All programs of fitness are based on the principle that in order to increase strength, muscles must be made to work harder than they normally do.

4. Exercise regularly. The second principle of fitness programs is that building and maintaining strength is dependent on regular activity. If your program is not regular, you will lose strength and muscle tone.

5. Gradually increase the number of repetitions, time periods of work, or amount of weight being lifted. You must continue overloading muscles as you become stronger.

6. Vary your program without losing the overall effect or resetting your goals. Many exercises are so boring that the people doing them lose interest. Use a variety of exercises, all of which help you achieve the same results.

7. Check with a physician before starting a program that is drastically more demanding than whatever you are doing now. Striving for fitness can kill you unless you know what you are doing. It is better to be a slightly less than fit human being than a wonderfully conditioned corpse.

IN CASE YOU GET HURT

Tennis fitness also encompasses the prevention and treatment of injuries. Although tennis elbow gets most of the publicity, there are several less serious but more common physical problems among tennis players. Blisters, sprains, strains, cramps, and shin splints are examples of tennis injuries almost all players have encountered.

Blisters

Beginning players and those who have not played for a while are probably going to have blisters on their racket hand and on their feet, in that order. A blister is an accumulation of fluid between the top two layers of skin. Blisters are caused by friction—in this case, friction between the racket and the hand, and between the foot and the sock, shoe, or court.

Some blisters can be avoided by following this advice: (1) Play for only short periods of time when you start and slowly increase the amount of playing time as you become physically tougher. The people who play tennis for two or three hours the first day out are certain to get blisters. (2) Make sure that your racket grip is the right size for you. Rackets with grips that are too large or too small will increase the amount of friction. (3) Keep the racket handle reasonably dry. The more slippage, the greater the chance of irritation to the hand. (4) Wear a tennis glove or tape on the areas of the hand most likely to blister. Although many players feel that they lose their touch if they have something between the hand and the racket, a glove may be worn until your hand becomes tough, then the glove will not be needed. (5) To avoid blisters on the feet, put talcum powder on your feet, wear shoes that fit, and wear two pairs of socks.

Once blisters develop, follow this procedure: Clean the area with alcohol or soap and water, sterilize a needle, and make an opening at the base of the blister so that the fluid can drain. Then place a bandage over the entire area. Some players can play with the pain caused by blisters and others cannot. Keep some first aid supplies with you at the courts, because the areas on the hands and feet likely to blister are difficult to bandage, and the bandages will come off as you move and perspire. In some cases, the top layer of skin should be removed, but this should be done by someone trained to do it correctly and safely.

Sprains

A sprain is an injury to a joint which usually damages blood vessels, ligaments, and tendons in the area. A sprain is frequently caused by forcing a joint beyond the normal range of motion. In tennis, the most common sprains occur in the ankles. If the ankle is sprained, the symptoms will be swelling, tenderness, pain upon motion or when weight is placed on the injured joint, and discoloration. It is possible for a fracture to occur at the same time as a sprain. The degree of pain should not be a factor in trying initially to determine whether or not a break has occurred. Sprains may be more painful than fractures.

If you sprain an ankle, do three things: Put pressure on the ankle with a wrap; put ice or some other cold application on the affected joint; and elevate the leg. All three first aid measures will reduce the amount of fluid rushing to the area, thus reducing the swelling and pain. Continue the cold applications until the swelling and bleeding subside. An elastic wrap will provide pressure without cutting off circulation. After the swelling and bleeding have stabilized, apply warm compresses to the area to stimulate circulation and healing.

Do not start playing too soon after a sprain. Joints sprained once seem to be more susceptible to subsequent sprains. When you do start playing, you may want to wrap or tape your ankle for support.

Strains

Strains are tears in muscle tissue and connective tissue. They may be caused by overexertion, sudden movement, fatigue, or improper warmup. In tennis, the most likely parts of the body to be affected by strains are the legs, back, and wrist. The symptoms will probably be sharp pain when the injured muscles are exercised, general soreness, and muscle spasms. Rest, heat, and massage are used to treat strains. Trainers, therapists, and physicians may treat pulled muscles by ultrasound and whirlpool bath methods. If the back muscles are involved, you should sleep on a firm surface so the sore muscles are not stretched further. If the wrist is strained, taping can give support and reduce the pain. The player who suffers a strain can usually begin to play sooner after the injury than the one who has a sprain.

Heat Cramps

Heat cramps usually affect tennis players in the legs, arms, or hands. The cramps are involuntary contractions of muscles, and they could be caused by fatigue, high temperature, loss of body salt, or overexertion of muscles. Pressure and warm wraps may alleviate the immediate discomfort, but many cramps could be avoided by progressive conditioning programs, adequate salt and water intake before and during periods of exercise, and rest periods while you play.

Shin Splints

A shin splint causes pain and discomfort in the lower leg. The injury may be an inflammation of the tissue between the two bones of the lower leg, an inflammation of muscles in that part of the leg, or a muscle spasm. Shin splints could be caused by running on hard surfaces, by playing on different kinds of surfaces, by poor conditioning, poor running techniques, or abnormalities in the skeletal structure.

You are more likely to suffer from shin splints when you first begin to play tennis regularly, especially if you play on a hard surface. The treatment for this kind of injury is taping to elevate and support the arch, using a foam rubber cushion in the heel of the shoe, taking aspirin before and after running, and soaking the leg in ice water for about fifteen minutes after running. If the pain is severe, the only other treatment is rest. Shin splints may be avoided by a thorough conditioning program so you can gradually adjust to playing conditions.

Tennis Elbow

Tennis elbow has been written about extensively in recent years, so there is much more information on the subject than will be presented here. One of the most thorough treatments of the subject appeared in the March 1974 issue of *Tennis* magazine. Causes, prevention, and cures are discussed in a series of articles.

Tennis elbow is an inflammation of the tissue around the end of the bone in the upper arm at the elbow. It could be caused by the constant impact of the ball on the racket, causing stress in the forearm muscles, by improper technique on certain strokes, by weak muscles, or by heavy and tightly strung rackets. The primary symptom of tennis elbow is pain in the elbow area. The pain may occur only on certain shots or in certain positions of the arm, but if the injury is serious enough, there may be pain to the touch and even pain when you shake hands with someone or brush your teeth.

There are many types of treatment, but no single method is effective for everyone. If you develop tennis elbow, get advice and treatment from a physician or therapist. Some of the treatment methods that have been successful include the use of cold packs to reduce inflammation, rest, medicines such as aspirin and cortisone, heat, massage, elbow braces, and even surgery. Middle-aged players account for more than half of those who get tennis elbow.

6

Practicing

PROBLEMS AND PATTERNS

There are several problems that tennis players face when it comes to practicing the game. For many, the problem is that there is just not enough time to practice and to play. These people may get to the courts or the club once or twice a week, and if they have to choose between practicing and playing, they would rather play. People in this group have to figure out a way to work in a concentrated practice session as part of the warmup before a match. Other players may be playing often enough to spend part of the time practicing, but they do not know how to spend their practice time in a way that will improve their game. Still others may have the time to practice, but no one with whom to practice; their problem is to learn how to put themselves through one-person practice sessions. Finally, there are players who have the time to practice, but who do not always have access to tennis courts. The weather may be bad, there may not be transportation to a tennis facility, they may have to stay home with children, or the courts may be reserved or full of other players. The solution to this problem is to develop a way to practice tennis at home. Each of these four practice problems will be discussed in this chapter.

Practice Problem Number 1:
"I Don't Have Time to Practice"

If you are the player who gets to play only once or twice a week, you must develop a very concentrated, systematic practice session into your pre-match warmup. You cannot afford to just go out and hit for a few minutes before starting your match. You have to work on specific strokes and situations that will carry over into the actual game. If you do not take the time to practice most of the strokes you are going to use, you cannot expect to hit those strokes consistently when play begins. Below is a ten-minute pre-match routine for two players. Your opponent is going to have to cooperate by participating in the same kind of warmup simultaneously. This routine is designed for intermediates; beginners should not be so anxious to spend all of their time playing.

TEN-MINUTE PRE-MATCH PRACTICE/WARMUP

2 minutes	General hitting; try to play every shot on the first bounce; move as much as you can to get into place for shots; run to pick up balls; stretch and loosen as many muscles as possible
2 minutes	Forehand groundstrokes; for the first minute try to hit shots down the line with your forehand while your opponent returns your shots with volleys down the same line; the other player practices volleys while you practice groundstrokes; during the second minute, you hit crosscourt with your forehand while your practice partner returns with crosscourt shots from a volleying position
2 minutes	Backhand groundstrokes; hit down the line the first minute and crosscourt the second minute; your opponent can stay at the net to hit more volleys or move to the baseline to practice groundstrokes
2 minutes	Volleys; now you practice your volleys while your opponent works on down-the-line and crosscourt groundstrokes; since there is a slight imbalance in the time both of you will spend practicing from the backcourt, work out a compromise based on who needs which kind of practice more
1 minute	One partner practices overhead smashes while the other practices the lob; alternate so that each player hits both kinds of shots
1 minute	Serve; you serve and let your opponent practice returns, or both players can alternate serving without returning shots with groundstrokes

Practice Problem Number 2:
"I Don't Know How to Practice"

If you have the time to practice, have someone to practice with, and have courts available on which to practice, your problem is the least serious of the four. Some of the principles that apply to physical fitness programs also apply to practicing tennis. First, make practicing enjoyable. One of tennis's great advantages over other sports is that it can be just as much fun to practice as it is to play. Setting goals for yourself is one way to make practice more interesting. How many serves can you get into the service court without a miss, or how many out of 25 can you put in? How many consecutive times can you and your partner keep the ball in play? How many consecutive volleys can you hit without a miss? How many backhands out of 25 can you put between the service line and the baseline? How many drop shots can you hit that bounce three times in front of the service line? If you decide to strive for goals, make your goals reasonably consistent with your ability. Competing with a friend as part of practicing is another interest-keeping technique. Keeping score on the number of "in" serves, overhead smashes returned, groundstrokes placed into areas of the court, or lobs hit into the backcourt are good ways to combine competition with repetition. Rewarding yourself with tennis equipment, accessories, or food might also make your practices more enjoyable and challenging. Keeping score by using the VASSS method, playing no-ad sets, and playing matches consisting of tie breakers only are other ways of making practice more fun.

Second, establish a regular time for practicing. Reserve at least one day a week for practice and do not let anyone talk you into a match. If you can play tennis every day, set aside more than one day a week to work on your strokes. Just as fitness depends on regularity, so do maintaining and improving your tennis game.

Designate part of each practice session as a time to develop or correct one special problem in your game. Work on all strokes during the practice period, but each day place particular emphasis on one stroke. Sometimes trying to accomplish too much with your total game in one period can be frustrating.

Use a variety of exercises, drills, and practice routines. They will be more fun if you have plenty of tennis balls. Start collecting them; the more you have in your ball basket, the less time you will have to spend picking them up. With a lot of balls to perform a lot of drills, you can avoid becoming bored from doing the same thing every time out. More than fifty drills were described in Chapter 2, "Learning the Strokes." Go back and pick some out that you like. Write them down and work out a time schedule for your next practice session. The drills you choose should vary, depending on your skill level.

If you are a beginner, try to find someone better than you who will occasionally practice with you by keeping the ball in play. If you practice with another beginner, try this one-hour practice routine:

ONE-HOUR PRACTICE ROUTINE FOR BEGINNERS

10 minutes	Short game; you and your practice partner each stand a few feet from opposite sides of the net; drop the ball and put it into play with a very light touch; keep the ball in play as long as you can up to five minutes; use forehand and backhand shots
10 minutes	You stay at the net and ask your partner to move back a few steps; while your partner continues to practice short groundstrokes, hold your racket up with a volley grip and present a target at which to hit; while your partner practices the forehand and backhand, you get to practice volleys; alternate roles after five minutes
10 minutes	Both players move back to the service lines and work on keeping the ball in play from that position; if you can control the ball, hit directly toward each other, then practice hitting crosscourt shots; alternate so that you hit to and from both sides; remember to keep the ball in play with the correct grip, but with a very shortened stroke
20 minutes	Take turns throwing balls to each other's forehand and backhand groundstrokes; the thrower should stand close to the net and the hitter should be just behind the service line; the hitter tries to direct the shot to the thrower; alternate so that both of you get to hit and throw for five minutes each on both strokes; if you have children, consider recruiting them to chase balls for you
10 minutes	Practice serves from the service line; if you can put eight out of ten serves into the proper court from that position, move back slightly; if you can do the same thing from there, move to the regular baseline serving position; serve from both the right and left sides; your partner can practice returning serves while you are serving; alternate roles after five minutes

If you are an intermediate, your practice sessions can be a bit more sophisticated, but do not try to do things you are not capable of doing. You will become discouraged very easily if you do. Get a basket of balls and adapt this one-hour practice to your needs:

ONE-HOUR PRACTICE ROUTINE FOR INTERMEDIATES

5 minutes	General hitting from the backcourt; hit everything after the first bounce
5 minutes	Forehand groundstroke versus backhand groundstroke down the line
5 minutes	Change sides; forehand versus backhand down the other line
5 minutes	Crosscourt forehands; try to place all shots between service line and baseline
5 minutes	Crosscourt backhands from opposite sides of the court
5 minutes	One player hits groundstrokes from the baseline area while the other hits volleys from a forecourt position
5 minutes	Same drill; change roles
5 minutes	Take turns lobbing and hitting overhead smashes
5 minutes	One player serves against the other, who practices the return of serve; serve from both sides
5 minutes	Same drill; change roles
10 minutes	Rally from the baselines; when a ball bounces in either player's forecourt, he or she hits a forcing shot down the line or down the middle and follows the shot to the net; the point is then played out as in a game situation; the first player to win five points wins the game

Here is one last suggestion for practice drills: try to design your own drills to simulate match situations. There are many shot sequences in tennis that occur over and over, and these sequences can easily be reproduced in practice. When you practice the situation, you are practicing something that is bound to happen in a match. If you can master the situation drills in practice, your match performance has to improve. Here are a few examples of combination drills for the beginning and intermediate players:

Singles Situation Drills

1. Player A serves; Player B returns the serve with a forehand or backhand groundstroke

2. Player A serves; Player B returns the serve with a lob

3. Player A serves; Player B returns with a short shot to the open side of the court

4. Player A drops a ball and hits down a line; Player B cuts the shot off at the net with a forehand or backhand volley

5. Player A hits a short shot to one side of the forecourt; Player B moves in and hits an approach shot down the line

6. Player A hits a short shot; Player B moves in and hits an approach shot; Player A returns with a lob

7. Player A hits a short shot; Player B moves in and hits an approach shot; Player A returns with a down-the-line groundstroke

8. Player A hits a forcing shot anywhere in the backcourt; Player B returns with a lob

9. Player A hits a lob; Player B returns with an overhead smash

10. Players A and B hit five to ten consecutive lobs without a miss; the ball must bounce between the service line and the baseline

11. Player A serves; Player B returns with a short shot; Player A hits a forcing shot and advances to the net

12. Players A and B station themselves at the service lines and hit consecutive volleys

13. Player A volleys from the net while Player B tries to pass Player A with groundstrokes

14. Player A positions himself or herself at the net; Player B lobs over A's head; Player A retreats to retrieve the lob

15. Player A hits a drop shot; Player B retrieves; Player A lobs over B's head

Doubles Situation Drills

1. Player A serves; Player B returns; Player C poaches and volleys to the open court or to Player D at the opposite service line

2. Player A serves; Player B returns with a lob over Player C at net; Player C smashes or moves to cover the other side of the court

3. Players A, B, C, and D exchange continuous volleys from positions near the service line

4. Player A serves; Player B returns crosscourt past Player C at the net

5. Player A serves; Player B returns crosscourt; Player A hits the third shot with a forcing groundstroke

6. Player A serves to Player B; Player B returns with a forcing shot and advances to the net with Player D

7. Players A and C stand behind one baseline and hit groundstrokes to Players B and D, who keep the ball in play with volleys (2 against 2)

8. With three players, Players A and B hit groundstrokes from the baseline to Player C, who keeps the ball in play with volleys (2 against 1)

9. With three players, Player A hits shots from the baseline to Players B and C, who stand near the net and keep the ball in play with volleys (1 against 2)

10. With three players, Players A and B lob to Player C, who smashes; A and B attempt to retrieve all shots

Practice Problem Number 3:
"I Don't Have Anyone to Practice With"

If you are this person, your options are limited. The number of ways a person can practice by oneself and not become bored are very few. If you have a basket of balls, you can always find an empty court and practice serving. Be sure to practice specific aspects of your serve, such as accuracy, form, or power. Use targets or strive for goals you have set. If you can find a tennis facility that will let you rent a ball-throwing machine, you can practice almost any stroke. Renting a machine at a club or at public courts is not usually expensive and you can get in more swings per minute than with any person you might practice with. If you have a child, husband, wife, or a friend who really owes you a favor, you might ask that person to be your human ball-throwing machine. Practicing against a wall or rebound net is another possibility for solo practice. Almost any stroke can be practiced, but it is difficult to concentrate for long periods of time using this method. The distance you stand from the wall and the force with which you hit should vary with your tennis ability.

Practice Problem Number 4:
"How Can I Practice at Home?"

The short answer to this question is, "You cannot." Actually, there are some possibilities. Most of the isotonic and isometric exercises mentioned in the previous chapter can be done at home. All of those swinging, lifting, pushing, pulling, and moving routines require no more than you, a weight, a racket, tennis ball, and a little space. A second way to practice at home is to watch your own strokes in a mirror. Of course you have to know what you are looking at and looking for, and you may not have reached that point yet.

If you have a big playroom or some outdoor space, you can practice tennis by working at closely related racket sports. You and your practice partner can use wooden paddles or racketball rackets to keep any kind of rubber ball or tennis ball in play. The similarities of hitting will help you maintain eye-hand coordination, reflex awareness, and racket control. There are some products available that can be used inside a house without the risk of breaking anything. If you have an outside wall to hit against, you can get in good practice and also release some of that tension built up by being inside all day. Rebound nets are available and are very effective for practicing groundstrokes, serves, and volleys. There are also possibilities for making up games to be played using rebound nets and boards. Playing at home is not like playing on a real court, but it is better than not playing tennis at all.

References

AARON, JAMES E., et al. *First Aid and Emergency Care.* New York: The Macmillan Company, 1972.

BARNABY, JOHN M. *Advantage Tennis: Racket Work, Tactics, and Logic.* Boston: Allyn and Bacon, Inc., 1975.

BROWN, ARLENE, and JIM BROWN. "A Woman's Guide to Beginning Tennis," *The Woman*, 10, no. 2 (June 1975), 110.

BROWN, JIM. "Seven Cardinal Sins of High School Tennis Players," *Scholastic Coach*, 41, no. 7 (March 1972), 68.

BROWN, JIM. "Thinking Lefthanded," *Scholastic Coach*, 42, no. 7 (March 1973), 68.

BROWN, JIM. *Tennis: Teaching, Coaching, and Directing Programs.* Englewood Cliffs, N.J.: Prentice-Hall, Inc., 1976.

CHAMBERLAIN, BRIAN, and JIM BROWN. "Anticipation and the Intermediate Tennis Player," *Athletic Journal*, 51, no. 9 (May 1972), 38.

GOULD, DICK. *Tennis, Anyone?* (2nd. ed.). Palo Alto, Calif.: National Press Books, 1971.

HELDMAN, JULIE. "Everything You Want to Know About Equipment," *World Tennis*, 21, no. 1 (June 1973), 16.

HENKEL, BARBARA, *et al. Foundations of Health Science.* Boston: Allyn and Bacon, Inc., 1971.

National Sporting Goods Association. *Tennis Facts.* Chicago: The Association, 1973.

POWELL, NICK. *The Code.* Princeton, N.J.: United States Lawn Tennis Association, 1974.

SEGURA, PANCHO, and GLADYS HELDMAN. "Getting in Shape," *World Tennis,* 23, no .2 (July 1975), 48.

TALBERT, WILLIAM F., and BRUCE S. OLD. *The Game of Singles in Tennis.* Philadelphia and New York: J.B. Lippincott Company, 1962.

Index